Microsoft® SharePoint® 2013: Site User

Microsoft® SharePoint® 2013: Site User

Part Number: 091107
Course Edition: 1.3

Acknowledgements

PROJECT TEAM

Author	Media Designer	Content Editor
Robert Carver	Alex Tong	Michelle Farney

Notices

DISCLAIMER

While Logical Operations, Inc. takes care to ensure the accuracy and quality of these materials, we cannot guarantee their accuracy, and all materials are provided without any warranty whatsoever, including, but not limited to, the implied warranties of merchantability or fitness for a particular purpose. The name used in the data files for this course is that of a fictitious company. Any resemblance to current or future companies is purely coincidental. We do not believe we have used anyone's name in creating this course, but if we have, please notify us and we will change the name in the next revision of the course. Logical Operations is an independent provider of integrated training solutions for individuals, businesses, educational institutions, and government agencies. Use of screenshots, photographs of another entity's products, or another entity's product name or service in this book is for editorial purposes only. No such use should be construed to imply sponsorship or endorsement of the book by, nor any affiliation of such entity with Logical Operations. This courseware may contain links to sites on the internet that are owned and operated by third parties (the "External Sites"). Logical Operations is not responsible for the availability of, or the content located on or through, any External Site. Please contact Logical Operations if you have any concerns regarding such links or External Sites.

TRADEMARK NOTICES

Logical Operations and the Logical Operations logo are trademarks of Logical Operations, Inc. and its affiliates.

Microsoft® SharePoint® 2013, Microsoft® Office 2013, Microsoft® Windows® 8, Microsoft® Office Web Apps, Microsoft® Word, Microsoft® Excel®, Microsoft® PowerPoint®, Microsoft® Outlook®, and Microsoft® OneNote® are registered trademarks of Microsoft Corporation in the U.S. and other countries. The other Microsoft products and services discussed or described may be trademarks or registered trademarks of Microsoft Corporation. The Facebook and Twitter products and services discussed or described may be trademarks or registered trademarks of Facebook and Twitter, respectively. All other product and service names used may be common law or registered trademarks of their respective proprietors.

Copyright © 2016 Logical Operations, Inc. All rights reserved. Screenshots used for illustrative purposes are the property of the software proprietor. This publication, or any part thereof, may not be reproduced or transmitted in any form or by any means, electronic or mechanical, including photocopying, recording, storage in an information retrieval system, or otherwise, without express written permission of Logical Operations, 3535 Winton Place, Rochester, NY 14623, 1-800-456-4677 in the United States and Canada, 1-585-350-7000 in all other countries. Logical Operations' World Wide Web site is located at www.logicaloperations.com.

This book conveys no rights in the software or other products about which it was written; all use or licensing of such software or other products is the responsibility of the user according to terms and conditions of the owner. Do not make illegal copies of books or software. If you believe that this book, related materials, or any other Logical Operations materials are being reproduced or transmitted without permission, please call 1-800-456-4677 in the United States and Canada, 1-585-350-7000 in all other countries.

Microsoft® SharePoint® 2013: Site User

Lesson 1: Accessing and Navigating SharePoint Team Sites 1
    Topic A: Access SharePoint Sites..2
    Topic B: Navigate SharePoint Sites... 9

Lesson 2: Working with Documents, Content, and Libraries... 25
    Topic A: Upload Documents... 26
    Topic B: Search for Documents and Files..................................... 37

Lesson 3: Working with Lists 49
    Topic A: Add List Items... 50
    Topic B: Modify List Items...55
    Topic C: Configure List Views... 62
    Topic D: Filter and Group with List Views......................................71

Lesson 4: Configuring Your SharePoint Profile 79
    Topic A: Update and Share Your Profile Information..................... 80
    Topic B: Share and Follow SharePoint Content............................. 84
    Topic C: Create a Blog.. 96

Lesson 5: Integrating with Microsoft Office 105

Topic A: Access and Save SharePoint Documents with Microsoft Office. 106

Topic B: Manage Document Versions through Office 2013 109

Topic C: Access SharePoint Data from Outlook 2013 117

Lesson 6: Working Offline and Remotely with SharePoint 125

Topic A: Synchronize Libraries, Sites, and MySite and Working Offline.. 126

Topic B: Work from a Mobile Device 133

Appendix A: Microsoft Office SharePoint 2013 Exam 77-419 139

Glossary 143

Index 147

About This Course

In many professional environments today, people work collaboratively in teams. Information technology and applications facilitate this by allowing people to easily share, access, edit, and save information. Microsoft® SharePoint® 2013 is a platform specifically designed to facilitate collaboration, allowing people to use familiar applications and Web based tools to create, access, store, and track documents and data in a central location. In this course, you will learn about and use a SharePoint Team Site to access, store, and share information and documents.

SharePoint is a complex platform with many features and capabilities. A strong understanding of those features and capabilities will allow you to work more efficiently and effectively with SharePoint, and with the documents and data stored in SharePoint. Furthermore, effective use of new social networking capabilities will allow you to identify, track and advance issues and topics most important to you, and collaborate with colleagues more effectively.

Course Description

Target Student

This course is designed for existing Microsoft Windows and Microsoft Office users who are transitioning to a SharePoint environment, who will need to access information and collaborate with team members on a Microsoft SharePoint team site.

Course Prerequisites

To ensure your success in this course you should be have basic end-user skills with Microsoft Windows 8 and any or all of the Microsoft Office 2007, 2010 or 2013 suite components, plus basic competence with Internet browsing. You can obtain this level of skills and knowledge by taking the following Logical Operations courses:

- *Using Microsoft® Windows® 8* or *Microsoft® Windows® 8 Transition from Windows® 7*
- Any or all of the courses in the Microsoft Office 2007, 2010, or 2013 curriculum.

Course Objectives

Upon successful completion of this course, knowledge workers in a variety of business environments will be able to effectively utilize resources on a typical SharePoint team site in the course of performing normal business tasks.

You will:

- Access and navigate SharePoint content.
- Add, upload, modify, search for, and preview documents in document libraries.
- Add and modify items in lists, configure list views, and filter and group lists.

- Create and update your profile; tag, share, and follow content on your personal sites; and create and manage a personal blog.
- Access, create, save, and manage document versions and synchronize data with Microsoft Office applications.
- Synchronize SharePoint data, work offline, and access data from a mobile device.

The LogicalCHOICE Home Screen

The LogicalCHOICE Home screen is your entry point to the LogicalCHOICE learning experience, of which this course manual is only one part. Visit the LogicalCHOICE Course screen both during and after class to make use of the world of support and instructional resources that make up the LogicalCHOICE experience.

Log-on and access information for your LogicalCHOICE environment will be provided with your class experience. On the LogicalCHOICE Home screen, you can access the LogicalCHOICE Course screens for your specific courses.

Each LogicalCHOICE Course screen will give you access to the following resources:

- eBook: an interactive electronic version of the printed book for your course.
- LearnTOs: brief animated components that enhance and extend the classroom learning experience.

Depending on the nature of your course and the choices of your learning provider, the LogicalCHOICE Course screen may also include access to elements such as:

- The interactive eBook.
- Social media resources that enable you to collaborate with others in the learning community using professional communications sites such as LinkedIn or microblogging tools such as Twitter.
- Checklists with useful post-class reference information.
- Any course files you will download.
- The course assessment.
- Notices from the LogicalCHOICE administrator.
- Virtual labs, for remote access to the technical environment for your course.
- Your personal whiteboard for sketches and notes.
- Newsletters and other communications from your learning provider.
- Mentoring services.
- A link to the website of your training provider.
- The LogicalCHOICE store.

Visit your LogicalCHOICE Home screen often to connect, communicate, and extend your learning experience!

How to Use This Book

As You Learn

This book is divided into lessons and topics, covering a subject or a set of related subjects. In most cases, lessons are arranged in order of increasing proficiency.

The results-oriented topics include relevant and supporting information you need to master the content. Each topic has various types of activities designed to enable you to practice the guidelines and procedures as well as to solidify your understanding of the informational material presented in the course. Procedures and guidelines are presented in a concise fashion along with activities and discussions. Information is provided for reference and reflection in such a way as to facilitate understanding and practice.

Data files for various activities as well as other supporting files for the course are available by download from the LogicalCHOICE Course screen. In addition to sample data for the course exercises, the course files may contain media components to enhance your learning and additional reference materials for use both during and after the course.

At the back of the book, you will find a glossary of the definitions of the terms and concepts used throughout the course. You will also find an index to assist in locating information within the instructional components of the book.

As You Review

Any method of instruction is only as effective as the time and effort you, the student, are willing to invest in it. In addition, some of the information that you learn in class may not be important to you immediately, but it may become important later. For this reason, we encourage you to spend some time reviewing the content of the course after your time in the classroom.

As a Reference

The organization and layout of this book make it an easy-to-use resource for future reference. Taking advantage of the glossary, index, and table of contents, you can use this book as a first source of definitions, background information, and summaries.

Course Icons

Watch throughout the material for these visual cues:

Icon	Description
	A **Note** provides additional information, guidance, or hints about a topic or task.
	A **Caution** helps make you aware of places where you need to be particularly careful with your actions, settings, or decisions so that you can be sure to get the desired results of an activity or task.
	LearnTO notes show you where an associated LearnTO is particularly relevant to the content. Access LearnTOs from your LogicalCHOICE Course screen.
	Checklists provide job aids you can use after class as a reference to performing skills back on the job. Access checklists from your LogicalCHOICE Course screen.
	Social notes remind you to check your LogicalCHOICE Course screen for opportunities to interact with the LogicalCHOICE community using social media.

Accessing and Navigating SharePoint Team Sites

Lesson Time: 45 minutes

Lesson Objectives

In this lesson, you will:

- Describe fundamental SharePoint team site structure, versions, and permissions, and access a SharePoint team site.

- Identify the navigation elements and features of a Microsoft SharePoint team site.

Lesson Introduction

In this course, you will create and edit content on a SharePoint team site, as well as create your own SharePoint MySite, and access SharePoint through Microsoft® Office applications. Before you can perform these tasks, you need to understand how collaboration software works in general and the specific capabilities and features of Microsoft® SharePoint® 2013. In this lesson, you will identify the basic functions and capabilities of collaboration software and SharePoint 2013 team sites. You will also access your SharePoint team site for the course and use SharePoint navigation controls to access your team site.

At its heart, SharePoint is a website. It is a website with a special framework and a rich set of features that allow people to share many different types of information easily. It allows coworkers to share documents much like server based file shares, but, because it is web-based, it offers many additional features. These features include the ability to have a team calendar or task list, rich viewing of media content such as videos, and version control for documents that are co-authored by multiple team members. SharePoint allows businesses to collaborate on documents and social networking, manage portals and websites, and provides content management, governance, and business intelligence analytical capabilities. In order to get the most out of SharePoint as a user, you must understand the fundamental technologies and capabilities of SharePoint.

TOPIC A

Access SharePoint Sites

SharePoint team sites run on SharePoint servers that are managed by the company Information Technology (IT) department. Before you can start using SharePoint, you have to access the SharePoint site.

The primary tools for accessing SharePoint are your web browser and Microsoft Office applications, such as Word, Excel® and PowerPoint®. In your work environment, your IT department or supervisor will provide you with information about how to access your company resources, including SharePoint sites. In order to get the most out of SharePoint as a user, you must understand the fundamental technologies and capabilities of SharePoint.

Collaboration Technology

Collaboration technology allows colleagues to effectively work together to achieve a common goal. Collaboration technologies store and provide centralized access to information such as documents, lists, media content, and other data that the team needs. In addition to providing centralized access to this information, it provides document management, integration with software applications, and tools used by team members, and other capabilities that make information sharing easier. Collaboration technologies are usually web-based and accessed on the corporate intranet or over the Internet.

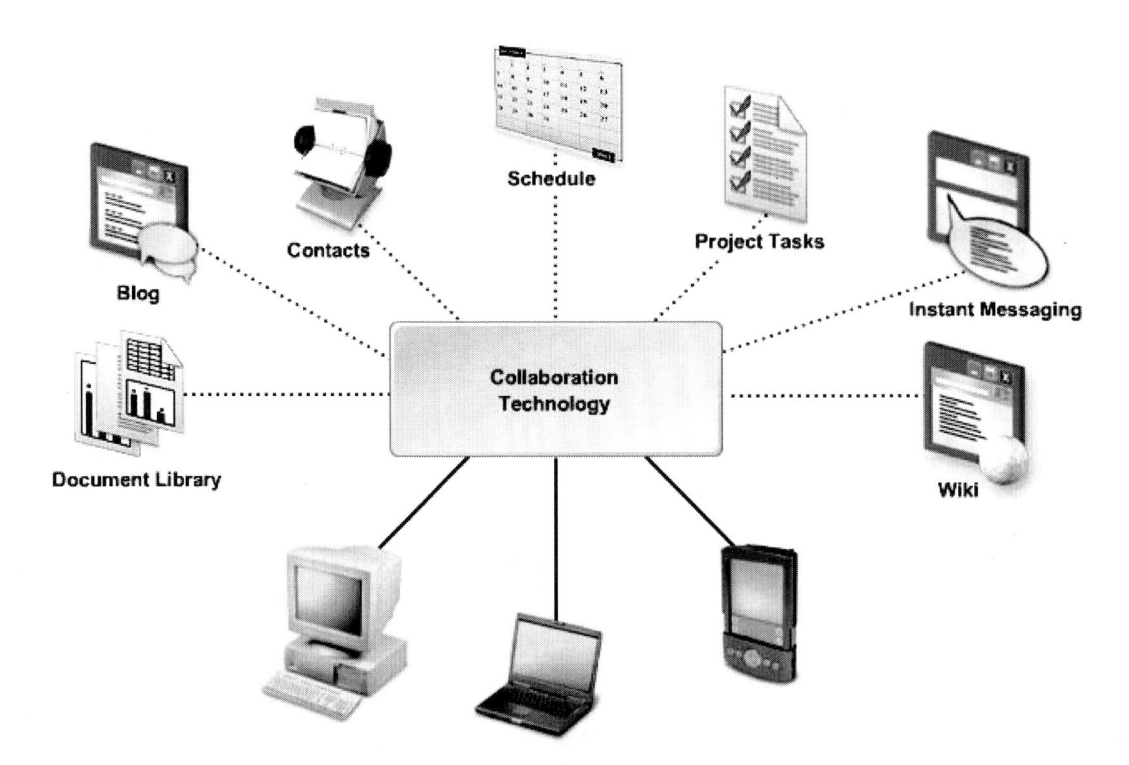

Figure 1-1: Collaboration technology.

SharePoint

Microsoft *SharePoint* 2013 is Microsoft's web-based business collaboration platform. This is a software product that allows people working as a team to share documents and other information, as well as to communicate with each other. SharePoint stores documents, spreadsheets, presentations, contact lists, calendars, and media content in a central web-based location. It also provides access control, content management and organization, file versioning, as well as options for checking content in and out. SharePoint integrates with popular social media such as Facebook, Twitter, and Yammer allowing users to collaborate across those social media networks. SharePoint sites are accessed with a web browser and content is opened and edited with productivity software such as Microsoft® Word or Excel.

SharePoint Integration, Offline and Enterprise Features

SharePoint integrates with Microsoft Office applications by allowing users to save and open documents directly from those applications to SharePoint sites. Users can make SharePoint sites available for offline use so that they can work when disconnected from the Internet, and synchronize changes when they come back online. The Enterprise version of SharePoint also offers content governance and business intelligence features which allows organizations and users to better utilize the content.

SharePoint Versions

There are multiple versions of SharePoint 2013. As a user, you don't have control of which version of SharePoint your organization has implemented, but to get the most out of SharePoint you should have a basic understanding of different versions of SharePoint.

There are currently five product variants in the SharePoint product line.

Version	Description
Microsoft SharePoint Foundation	This is the most basic version of SharePoint and offers broad, centralized collaboration capabilities, built-in features, integration with Microsoft Office and content management capabilities.
Microsoft SharePoint Server Standard	This version provides the features available in SharePoint Foundation as well as many enhanced and additional features such as social networking integration, additional content management options, workflow features, and improvements in search.
Microsoft SharePoint Server Enterprise	This version provides the features in SharePoint Server Standard as well as enhanced and additional features in business intelligence, records management, and eDiscovery.
Microsoft SharePoint Designer	This version is a separate tool that provides enhanced web design capabilities that allow you to customize the look, feel, and navigation of your SharePoint site.
Microsoft SharePoint Online and Office 365™	These are online variants of SharePoint that allow organizations to use SharePoint features, but the SharePoint servers are maintained in the cloud. SharePoint online versions vary depending on the service plan with which they are associated.

SharePoint Sites

SharePoint sites are websites that run on a SharePoint server and offer the collaboration features and capabilities provided by SharePoint. At the most fundamental level, SharePoint sites are websites accessed most commonly through browsers. Your supervisor, HR contact, or IT contact should provide you with a URL and user account that allows you to access the SharePoint sites that you will be working with. You may also access SharePoint features or documents stored in SharePoint through Microsoft Office applications. This access should be configured for you, and you should receive instructions on how to access documents stored in SharePoint through your Office applications.

SharePoint Groups

Access to SharePoint sites, whether you can open the site, and what actions you can take in a site, are determined by permissions that have been associated with a group or user account. Typically user accounts are added to one of the following three *SharePoint groups* (most commonly, the members group) to provide access rights. The bottom line is that you should have the ability to perform the tasks in SharePoint that are required for your job. If you do not, contact your supervisor or IT support staff and ask them to help.

Group	Access Rights
Visitors	Have permissions to view and read content.
Members	Have permissions to read, contribute, modify and delete site content.
Owners	Have the same permissions as members and additional permissions to approve content, create new sites and structures, and modify the overall site.

SharePoint Permission Levels

Permission levels are rights that are granted to users or groups that provide access to, and allow you to perform actions on a SharePoint site. Administrators assign default permissions to users and groups, or may choose to customize permissions. The following table lists the default permissions in SharePoint 2013. Depending on the site template used to create the SharePoint site (i.e. Team site or Publishing site), some permission levels may not be available.

Permission Level	Description	Permissions Included by Default
View Only	Enables users to view application pages. The View Only permission level is used for the Excel Services Viewers group.	• View Application Pages • View Items • View Versions • Create Alerts • Use Self Service Site Creation • View Pages • Browse User Information • Use Remote Interfaces • Use Client Integration Features • Open
Limited Access	Enables users to access shared resources and a specific asset. Limited Access is designed to be combined with fine-grained permissions to enable users to access a specific list, document library, folder, list item, or document, without enabling them to access the whole site. Limited Access cannot be edited or deleted.	• View Application Pages • Browse User Information • Use Remote Interfaces • Use Client Integration Features • Open

Permission Level	Description	Permissions Included by Default
Restricted Read	View pages and documents. Permission is for publishing sites only.	• View Items • Open Items • View Pages • Open
Read	Enables users to view pages and list items, and to download documents.	Limited Access permissions, plus: • View Items • Open Items • View Versions • Create Alerts • Use Self-Service Site Creation • View Pages
Contribute	Enables users to manage personal views, edit items and user information, delete versions in existing lists and document libraries, and add, remove, and update personal Web Parts.	Read permissions, plus: • Add Items • Edit Items • Delete Items • Delete Versions • Browse Directories • Edit Personal User Information • Manage Personal Views • Add/Remove Personal Web Parts • Update Personal Web Parts
Edit	Enables users to manage lists.	Contribute permissions, plus: • Manage Lists
Approve	Edit and approve pages, list items, and documents. For publishing sites only.	Contribute permissions, plus: • Override List Behaviors • Approve Items
Design	Enables users to view, add, update, delete, approve, and customize items or pages on the website.	Edit permissions, plus: • Add and Customize Pages • Apply Themes and Borders • Apply Style Sheets • Override List Behaviors • Approve Items
Manage Hierarchy	Create sites; edit pages, list items, and documents, and change site permissions. For Publishing sites only.	Design permissions minus the Approve Items, Apply Themes and Borders, and Apply Style Sheets permissions, plus: • Manage permissions • View Web Analytics Data • Create Subsites • Manage Alerts • Enumerate Permissions • Manage Web Site
Full Control	Enables users to have full control of the website.	All permissions.

> **Note:** Additional information on permissions levels can be found on Microsoft Technet at: http://technet.microsoft.com/en-us/library/cc721640.aspx.

> Access the Checklist tile on your CHOICE Course screen for reference information and job aids on **How to Access a SharePoint Site**.

ACTIVITY 1-1
Accessing Your SharePoint Team Site

Before You Begin
You should be at your classroom workstation; you should not be logged in; and there should be nothing running on the client.

Scenario
Develetech is a manufacturer of home electronics. Develetech is known as an innovative designer and producer of high-end televisions, video game consoles, laptop and tablet computers, and mobile phones. Develetech is a mid-sized company, employing approximately 2,000 residents of Green City and the surrounding area. Develetech also contracts with a number of partner organizations for new product development as well as manufacturing and supply-chain support.

You have been hired as a software developer at Develetech. The development team writes software that ships with its manufactured products. The software spans a wide range of uses including setup and programming software for the devices, add-in software, games, as well as management and control software.

The team uses SharePoint extensively as their primary collaboration tool. They use it for team communications, updates, announcements and events, and document sharing as well as project specific collaboration. As a new member of the team, you've been asked to verify that our new user account has the appropriate rights by accessing the development team SharePoint site.

> **Note:** Activities may vary slightly if the software vendor has issued digital updates. Your instructor will notify you of any changes.

1. Sign in to your computer.
   a) Press **Ctrl+Alt+Del** to log on to your student computer.
   b) In the **User Name** text box, type your user name.

c) In the **Password** text box, type *password12!* and press **Enter**.

2. Access the Develetech SharePoint server.
    a) On the Windows 8 Start page, select the **Desktop** tile.
    b) Open your web browser. A blank page is shown at startup.
    c) In the **Address box** type *http://sharepoint* and press **Enter**.
    d) Observe the **Develetech Developer Team Site**.

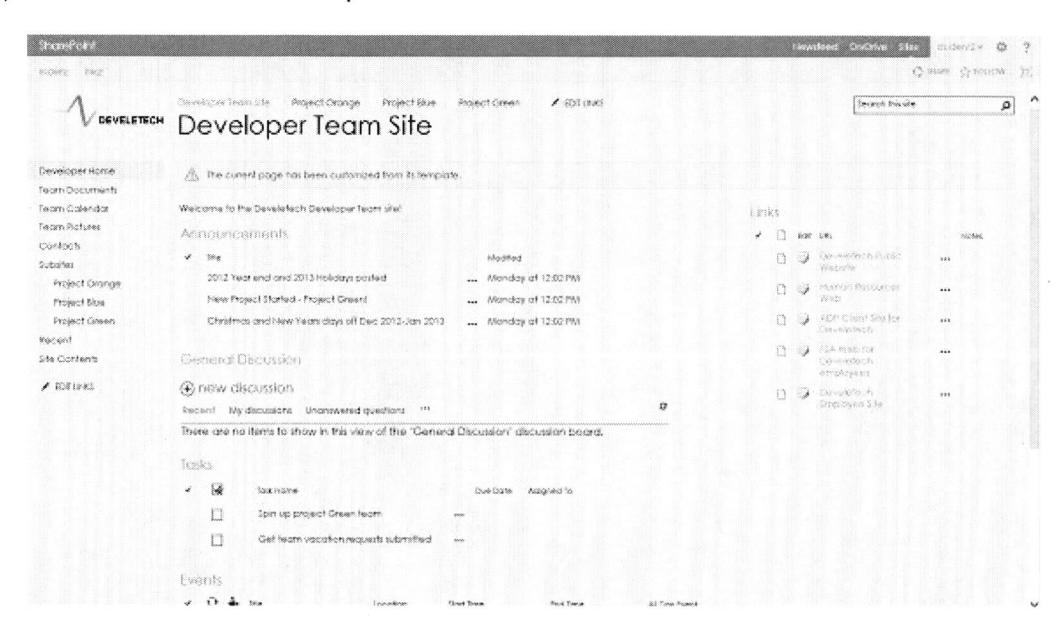

TOPIC B

Navigate SharePoint Sites

Now that you know how to access a SharePoint site, you should familiarize yourself with the user interface (UI) used by SharePoint. SharePoint uses a number of site elements to allow users to navigate around the site itself, access applications that are installed, and access the content and data exposed by those applications. In this topic, you will identify the navigation elements and features of a Microsoft SharePoint team site.

SharePoint Site Hierarchy

All SharePoint sites exist in a hierarchy. The top of the hierarchy is called the top-level site. The top-level site may have many subsites, including Team Sites, Project Sites, Document Workspace Sites, and Meeting Workspace Sites. The entire top-level site and all of its subsites are called a site collection. A site collection is a logical grouping of sites, such as a set of SharePoint sites for the finance department. A site collection has the same owner, administrative settings, security, navigation, and content structures. The permissions and navigation of the top-level site are often inherited by subsites but can also be managed independently. Site collections make administration easier. Administrators plan and implement site collections, top-level sites, and subsites carefully to provide the collaboration and management required by an organization.

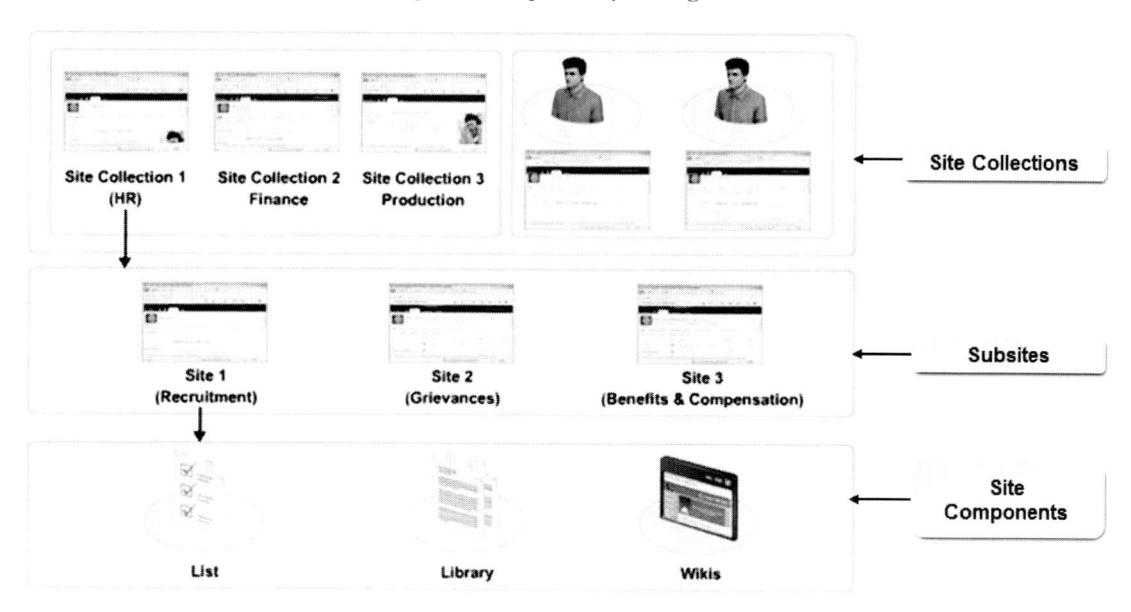

Figure 1-2: SharePoint site hierarchy.

SharePoint Team Sites

SharePoint team sites are a type of SharePoint site created using the Team Site template. Team sites are intended to facilitate communication and information sharing between team members. A team site can have subsites to accommodate different departments or working groups within a team. A team site has basic elements, such as a title and navigation tools, and will have a mix of SharePoint apps to accommodate team functions and responsibilities such as document sharing, social network interaction, calendars, and so forth. A team site may exist at the top-level of a SharePoint site, or may be a subsite of a top-level site.

SharePoint Windows 8 Style UI

One of the most noticeable changes in SharePoint 2013 from previous versions is the new user interface (UI). The interface is redesigned to be a Windows® 8 style UI. The Windows 8 style was formerly called the Metro style. The UI is simplified, offering blocky style graphics, and extensively uses typography, straight lines and whitespace. This makes SharePoint 2013 sites look different from SharePoint sites created in previous versions. Gone are the frames that section off the various portions of the UI, there is more blank space, and elements for navigation and application access are called out prominently.

SharePoint Interface Elements

Microsoft SharePoint provides a user interface (UI) that makes finding information and navigating SharePoint sites, pages, and apps easy. There are several interface elements that you should become familiar with and they are listed in the following table.

Figure 1-3: SharePoint interface elements.

Interface Element	Purpose
Header	The header spans the entire top of the page in a SharePoint site and provides access to several SharePoint features. On the right portion of the header, you can access your personal Newsfeed, OneDrive®, and MySite. On the far right of the header you can see the user account that you are logged into the site with, and access the **Settings** menu and **Help** button.
Ribbon	The ribbon allows you to perform tasks related to the site. You will see the **BROWSE** and **PAGE** tabs on the ribbon, and may see more depending on your role and permissions level. When you select a tab with commands available, the ribbon expands and command buttons become visible allowing you to easily perform those tasks. At the far right of the ribbon you can select the **FOLLOW** link to be updated when content changes occur. You can also select the **Focus on Content** button to hide navigation components from view.

Interface Element	Purpose
Top Links bar	At the top of the page, above the page title, is the Top Links bar. It may include links to lists, libraries, apps, the top-level site and subsites. Site administrators add links to the Top Links bar to allow users to easily navigate to those specific areas on the site. At the far right is the site search box where you can type search strings and search for content.
Page title	The Page title is the title of the current page and it appears just below the Top Links bar.
Quick Launch area	On the left side of the page is the **Quick Launch** area. This area contains links to other pages, subsites, and SharePoint lists, libraries, and apps that are frequently used. Administrators add links to the **Quick Launch** section to make it easier for users to navigate to popular areas of the site.
SharePoint lists, libraries, and apps	SharePoint apps are components that site owners and designers add to the site to provide a set of functionality for collaboration. For example, a SharePoint Document Library allows users to share documents.
Page section	This is the portion of the page where the content is displayed. The page section may be organized in a number different layouts with columns, sidebars, headers and footers. The various portions of the page will contain text, lists, libraries, and apps, and will allow you to access information, perform tasks and collaborate with co-workers.

The Header

The *header* spans the top of the pages and has several components that you should be aware of.

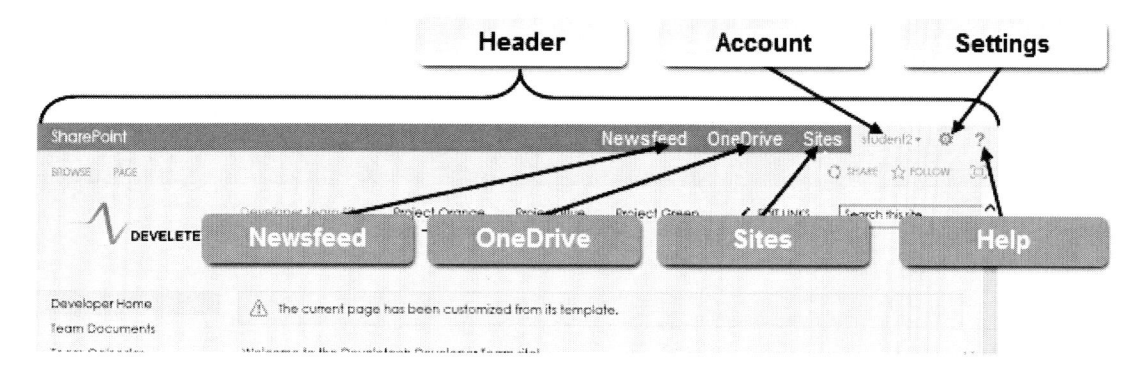

Figure 1-4: The header.

Header Component	Description
Newsfeed button	Accesses your personal newsfeed. The first time you select this button, your newsfeed is configured and you are prompted to share it with others. You will learn more about your newsfeed later.
OneDrive button	Accesses your personal OneDrive in the cloud and allows you to store and share files and data through OneDrive. The first time you select the **OneDrive** button, your OneDrive account is created and configured. The file sharing interface to OneDrive through SharePoint looks much like the Document Library interface.

Header Component	Description
Sites button	Accesses your MySite. A MySite is a personal SharePoint workspace that allows you to create your own personal collaboration space to work with your colleagues. The first time you select this button, your MySite will be created. You will learn more about MySites later.
Account	Displays the account that you are currently logged on with and displays a menu that allows you to sign out, and to view and update your SharePoint profile information by selecting **About Me**. You will learn more about your profile later.
Settings menu	Displays a menu that allows you to perform collection, site, and page level functions depending on your role and permissions level. Users may have the ability to share a page, or create or edit a new page. Site owners may have the ability to edit pages, change site settings, and change the look and feel of the site.
Help button	Displays the help window which allows you to browse help topics or search for key words in the help file.

The Ribbon

The *ribbon* provides several tabs, buttons, and components that allow you to perform tasks on SharePoint pages, apps, and content without the need for extensive navigation.

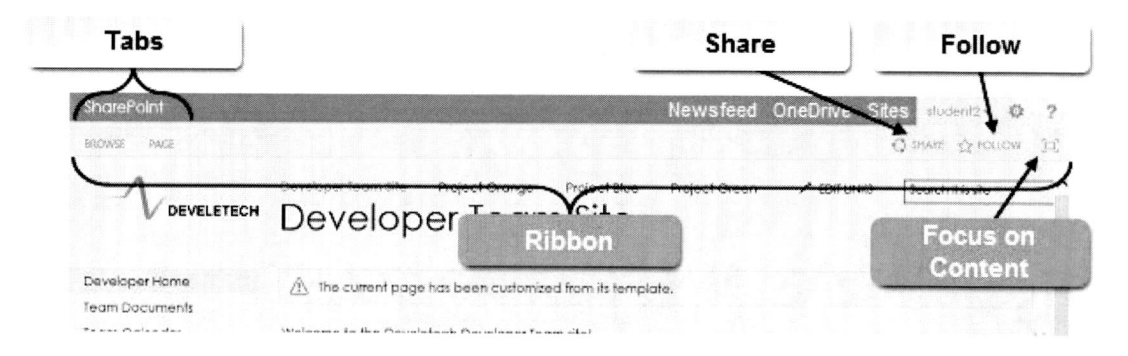

Figure 1-5: The ribbon.

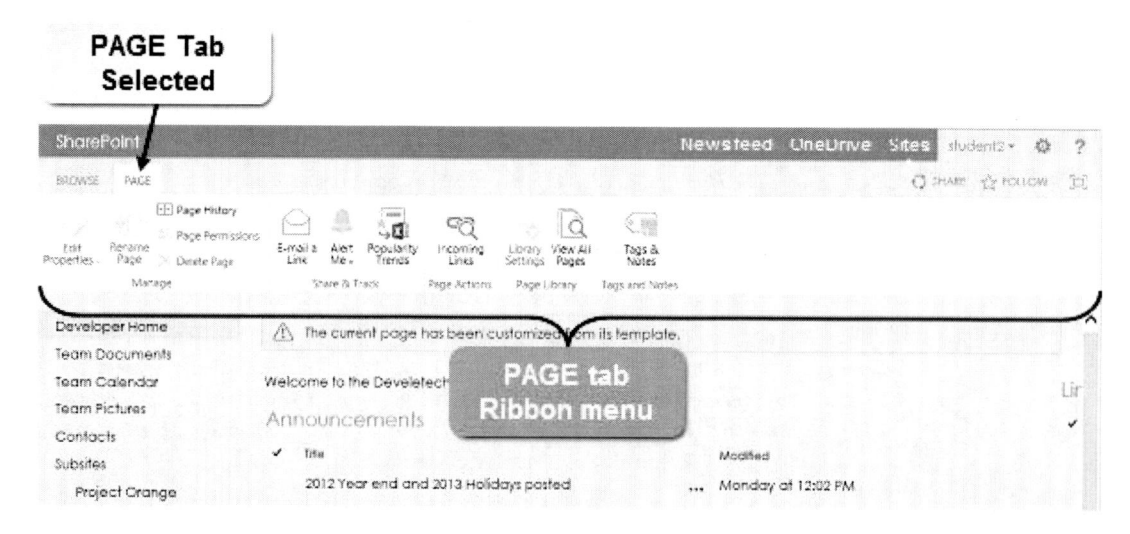

Figure 1-6: The ribbon with PAGE tab selected.

Ribbon Component	Description
BROWSE tab	Allows you to turn off other ribbon menus and return to browsing the SharePoint site. For example, if you had accessed other functions on the **PAGE** menu and were finished, you could select the **BROWSE** tab to collapse the **PAGE** ribbon and resume normal browsing.
PAGE tab	Displays the **PAGE** ribbon and associated buttons. This ribbon contains controls that allow you to perform page level tasks. The number of options available depends on your role and permissions level. Users often can only share links, view page history, and view popularity trends to see which content is most popular. Site administrators, on the other hand, may be able to edit and check out pages, as well as set permissions and adjust library settings.
SHARE button	Allows administrators with the appropriate permission level to assign users rights to access the page. This button is not visible if you do not have the appropriate permissions.
FOLLOW button	Allows you to follow the current page. Selecting this button adds a link to the current page to the **Sites I'm Following** section of your MySite. This allows you to quickly get back to pages you follow from your MySite.
EDIT button	Allows administrators and site designers with the appropriate permission level to edit the page. This button is not visible if you do not have the appropriate permissions.
Focus on Content button	Hides several navigation elements including the Top Links bar and search box, the page title, and **Quick Launch** area leaving only the page, and the content lists, libraries and apps visible so that you can focus on working with content. Select the button again to reveal these navigation elements.

The Quick Launch Area

The *Quick Launch* area provides several links to lists, libraries, apps, and pages on the site and allows you to navigate to those areas quickly. Site designers choose which lists, libraries, and apps to link to from the **Quick Launch** area.

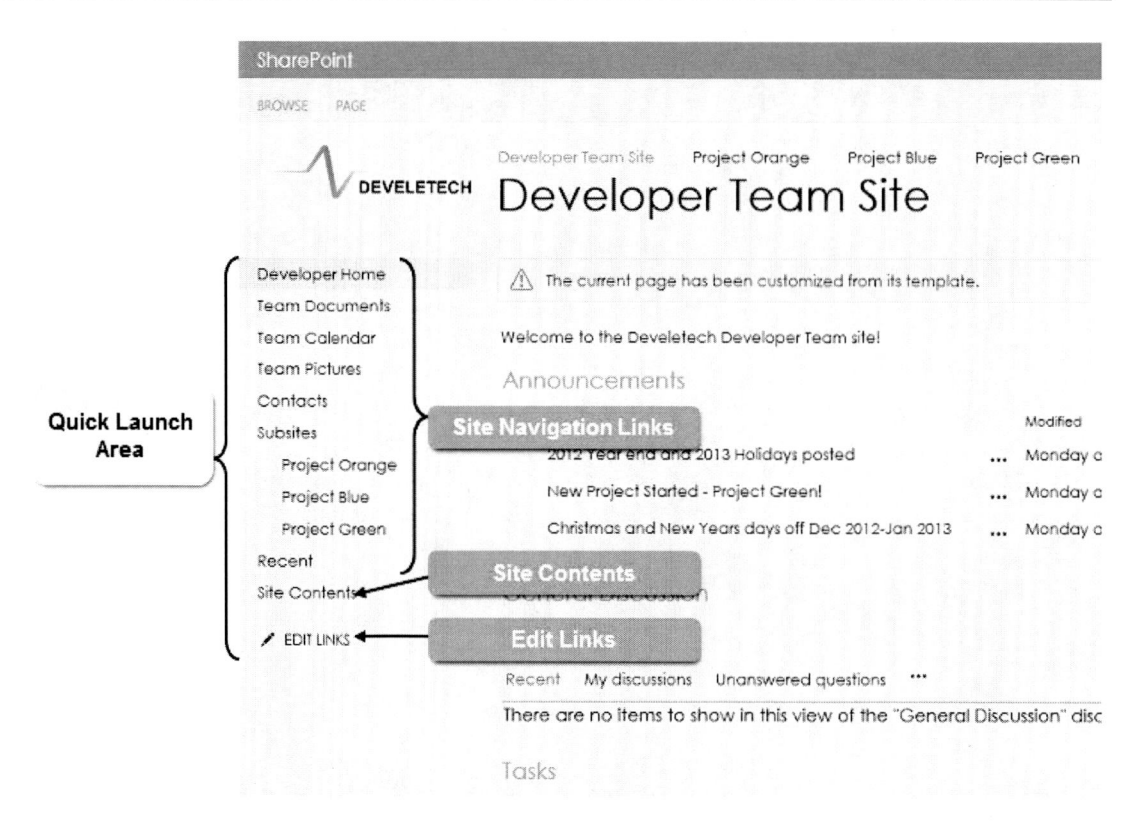

Figure 1-7: The Quick Launch area.

Quick Launch Area Component	Description
Site Navigation Links	Links to specific pages, lists, libraries, and apps on the site and potentially other sites. These links allow for quick navigation to commonly accessed content and information.
Site Contents Link	Displays all the lists, libraries, apps and subsites on the site. You can select any of them to go directly to the component you wish to use.
EDIT LINKS	Allows administrators and site designers to add, remove, edit, and reorder the links in the **Quick Launch** area. This link is not visible if you do not have the appropriate permissions.

The Page Section

The *page section* is the area of the page to the right of the **Quick Launch** area, under the header and the ribbon. The page section contains the content for that page on the SharePoint site. It can contain one or more SharePoint lists, libraries, and apps depending on how content is laid out for the site. You may find that all the page objects fit on the screen at the same time, or you may have to scroll left to right or down in order to see all the objects on the page. Site administrators and designers may organize content differently based on organizational and user needs. Get to know the layout of the SharePoint sites you use, and provide feedback to administrators and site designers if you feel the layout could be improved to make everyday tasks easier.

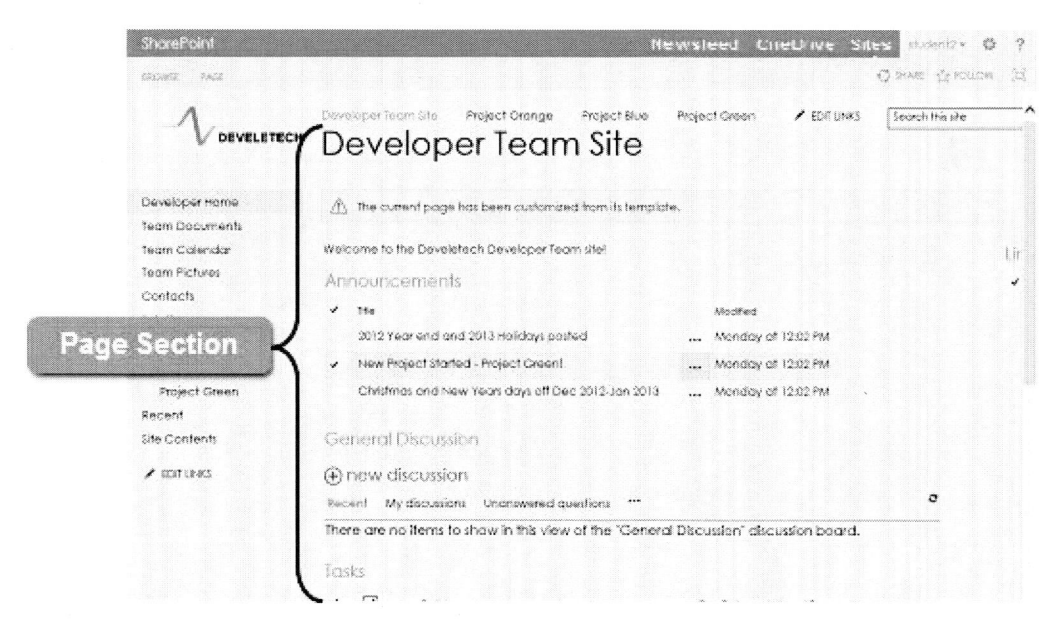

Figure 1-8: The page section.

SharePoint Lists, Libraries, and Apps

SharePoint provides components that can be added to your SharePoint site to enable a desired set of functionality. For example, a document library can be added so that a team has a central location to create, store, and update documents and files. There are several types of lists provided by SharePoint that allow users to keep track of tasks, record issues, even have discussions online. SharePoint also provides apps that offer different functionality, such as wiki pages and external data connection libraries. Libraries, lists and apps are the components of the Share Point site where most user interaction and collaboration takes place, where documents are shared, lists are updated, and discussions are engaged. When you are performing a task on a Share Point site, you will be accessing a library, list or app to do so.

> **Note:** To learn more about SharePoint Apps and the SharePoint Marketplace, refer to the LearnTO **Find and Add Apps from the SharePoint Apps Marketplace** presentation from the **LearnTO** tile on the LogicalCHOICE Course screen.

ACTIVITY 1-2
Navigating Your SharePoint Team Site

Before You Begin
You should be logged onto the classroom SharePoint site, and your browser should have the Developer Team Site page open.

Scenario
Now that you have access to the Develetech Developer Team site, your supervisor has asked you to familiarize yourself with the site, its lists, libraries, apps, and subsites so that you know where to look for information and how to collaborate with your coworkers.

1. Review lists, libraries, apps, and navigation components on the Develetech Developer Home Page.
   a) Observe the **Develetech Developer Team Site.**

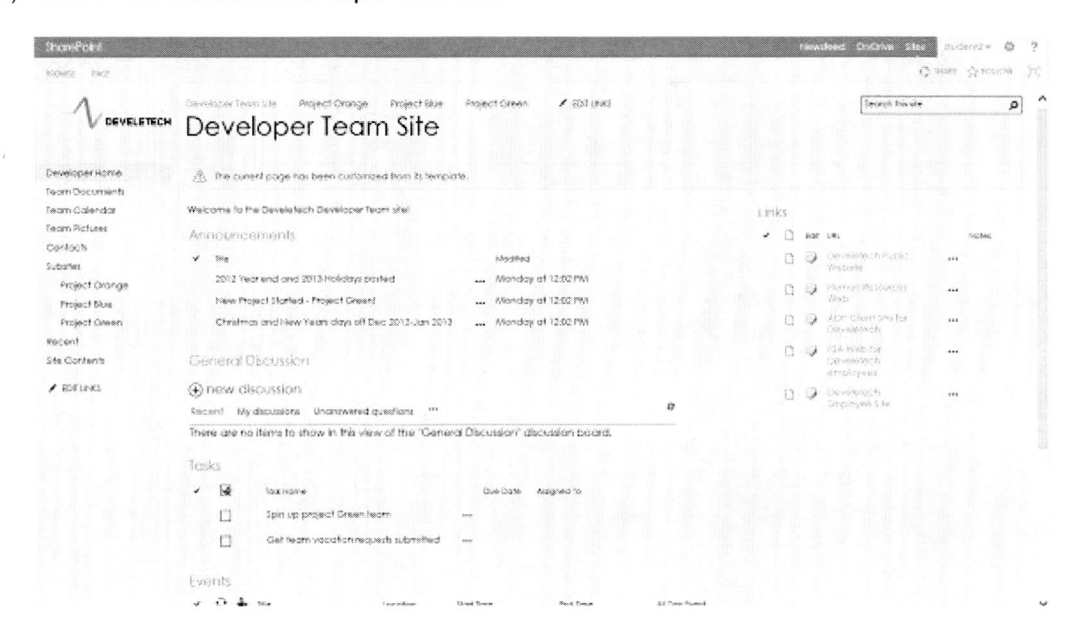

   b) Observe the links in the **Top Links** bar.

   > **Note:** The top links bar allows for navigation around the SharePoint site and is configured by the administrator or site owner. In this case the top links bar allows for navigation to the project sites which are subsites of the main site, and back to the home page for the site.

   c) Observe the page area and the lists, libraries, and apps that are visible on the **Developer Team Site** home page.

d) Observe the **Quick Launch** area and the links that are available there.

```
SharePoint
BROWSE    PAGE

        DEVELETECH

Developer Home
Team Documents
Team Calendar
Team Pictures
Contacts
Subsites
    Project Orange
    Project Blue
    Project Green
Recent
Site Contents

✎ EDIT LINKS
```

2. Review additional site components accessible from the **Quick Launch** area.

a) In the **Quick Launch** area, select **Team Documents** to open the Team Documents library.

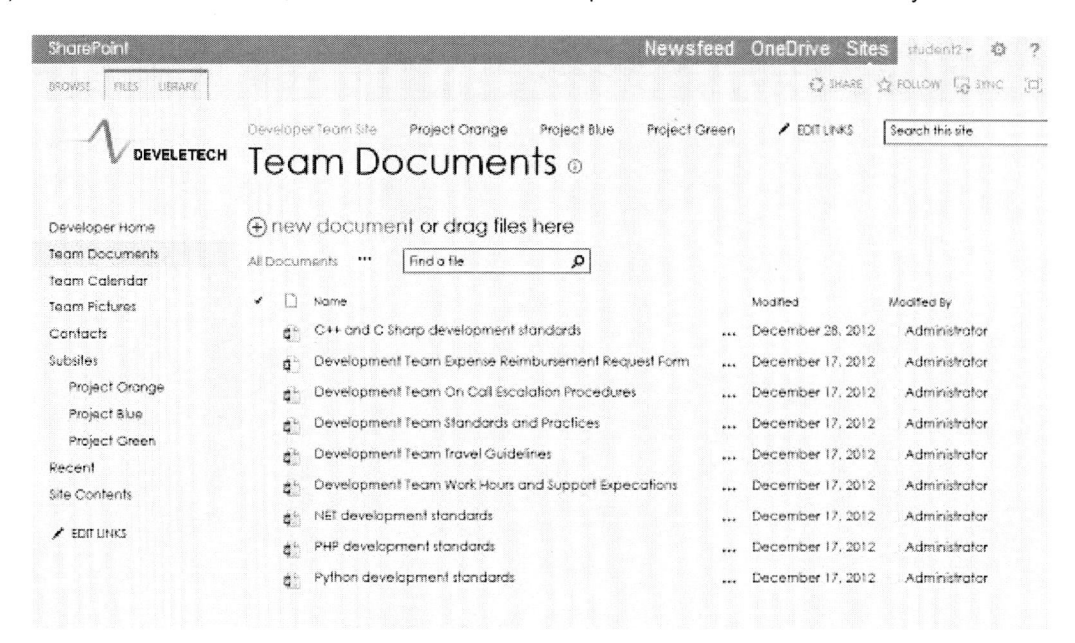

b) Review the content and options that are available in the Team Documents library.
c) In the **Quick Launch** area, select **Team Calendar** to open the Team Calendar list.

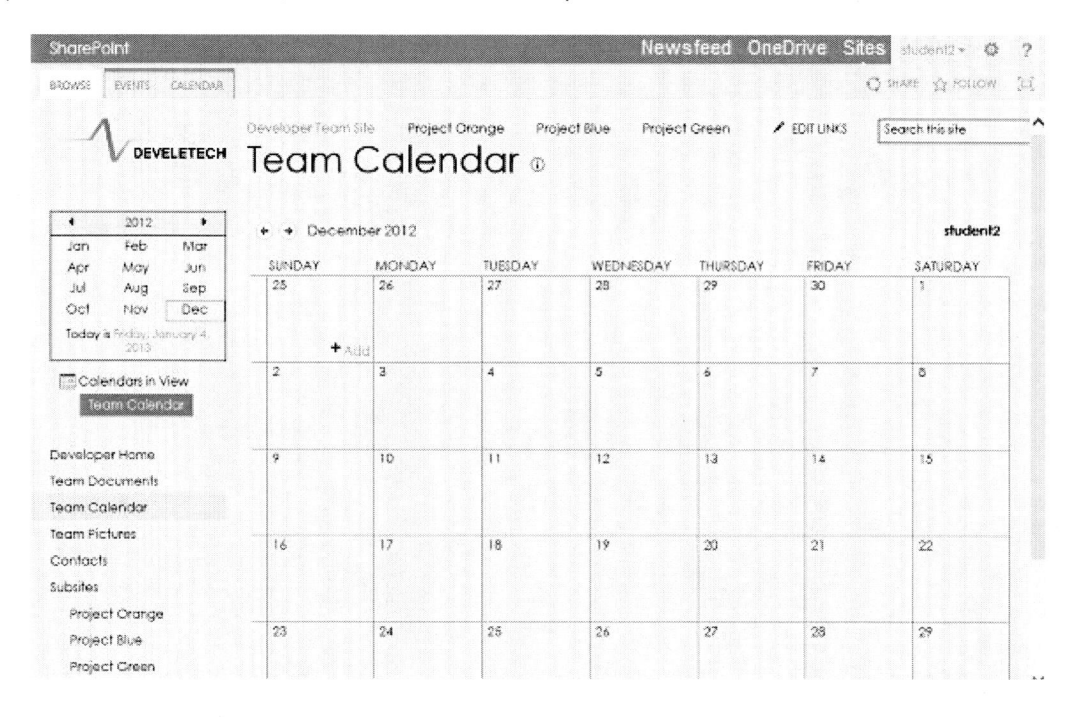

d) Review the content and options that are available in the Team Calendar list.

e) In the **Quick Launch** area, select **Contacts** to open the Contact list.

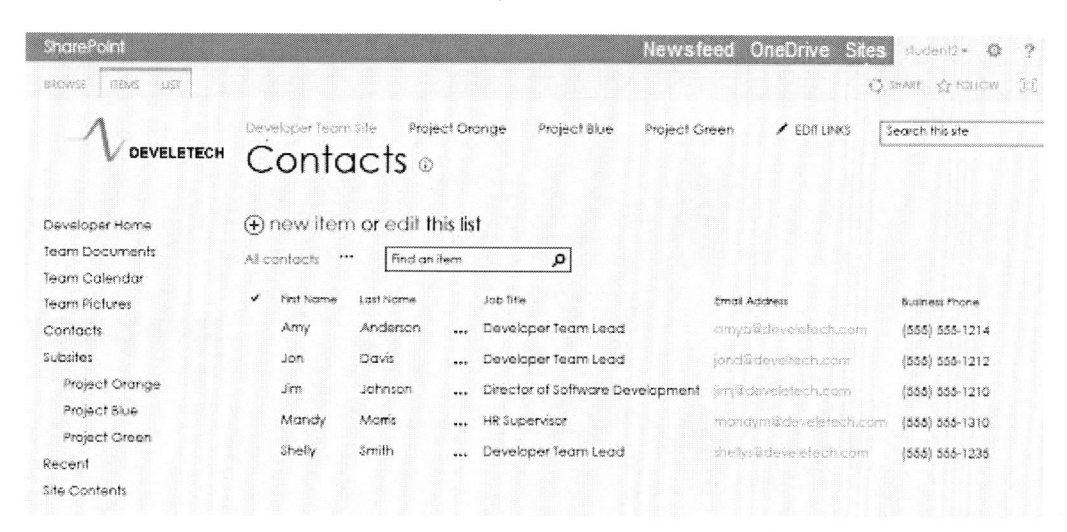

f) Review the content and options that are available in the Contacts list.
g) In the **Quick Launch** area, select **Site Contents** to open the **Site Contents** page.

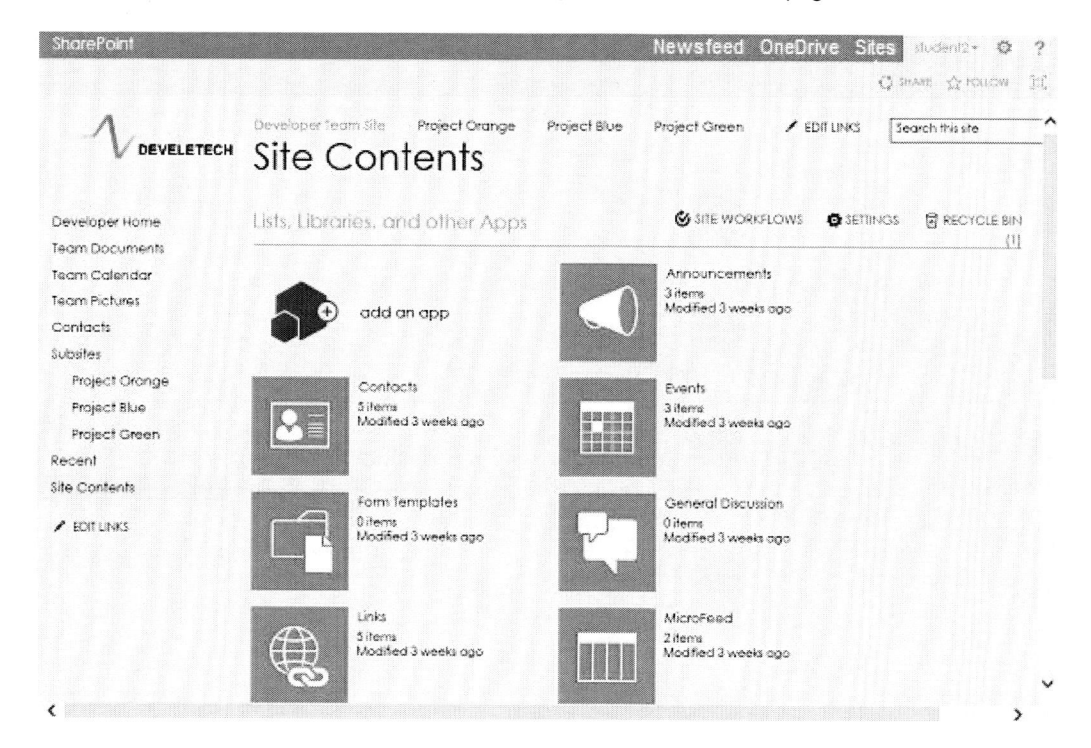

h) Scroll down and observe the lists, libraries, apps, and subsites that are part of the SharePoint site.

> **Note:** There are three subsites created in this site. Each subsite is set up to support a specific project and the project team.

3. Navigate to and review the Project Orange subsite.

a) In the **Quick Launch** area, under **Subsites,** select **Project Orange** to open the Project Orange subsite.

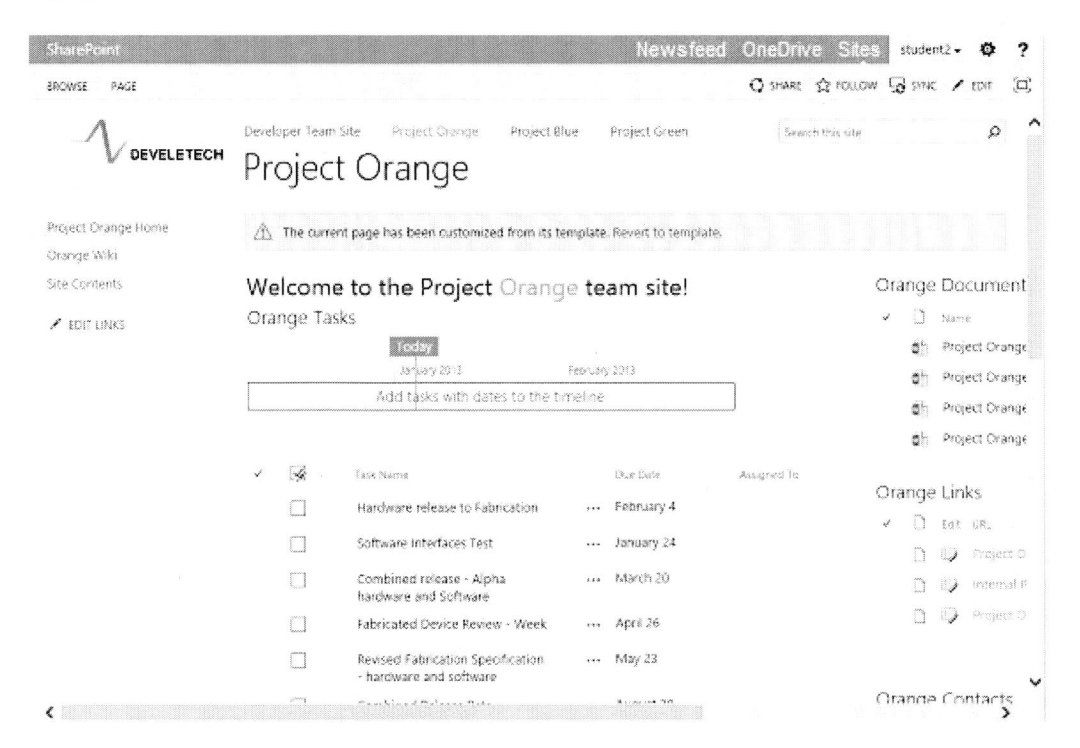

b) Observe the **Top Links** bar and note that it is the same as it was on the Developer Team Site page.
c) Observe the lists, libraries, and apps available on the Project Orange home page, as well as the links available in the **Quick Launch** area.
d) In the **Quick Launch** area, select **Site Contents** to open the **Site Contents** page.
e) Scroll down to view all the lists, libraries, apps, and subsites that are part of the SharePoint site.

4. Review the Project Blue and Project Green subsites.

> **Note:** The Project Orange, Blue, and Green sites are all identical. Develetech uses the same customized Team Site template for their project sites.

a) In the **Top Links** bar, select **Project Blue** to open the Project Blue subsite.
b) Observe that the Project Blue subsite is very similar to Project Orange.
c) In the **Top Links** bar, select **Project Green** to open the Project Green subsite.
d) Observe that the Project Green subsite is very similar to the Project Orange and Project Blue subsites.

5. Verify ribbon options and functionality.

a) In the **Top Links** bar, select **Developer Team Site** to return to the Developer Team Site page.

b) On the ribbon, select the **PAGE** tab to open the **PAGE** controls.
c) Observe the buttons that are available on the **PAGE** ribbon and those that are unavailable.
d) On the ribbon, select the **BROWSE** tab to close **PAGE** controls and return to site browsing.

6. Access and create your Newsfeed.

    a) On the header, select **Newsfeed** to configure and open your **Newsfeed** page.

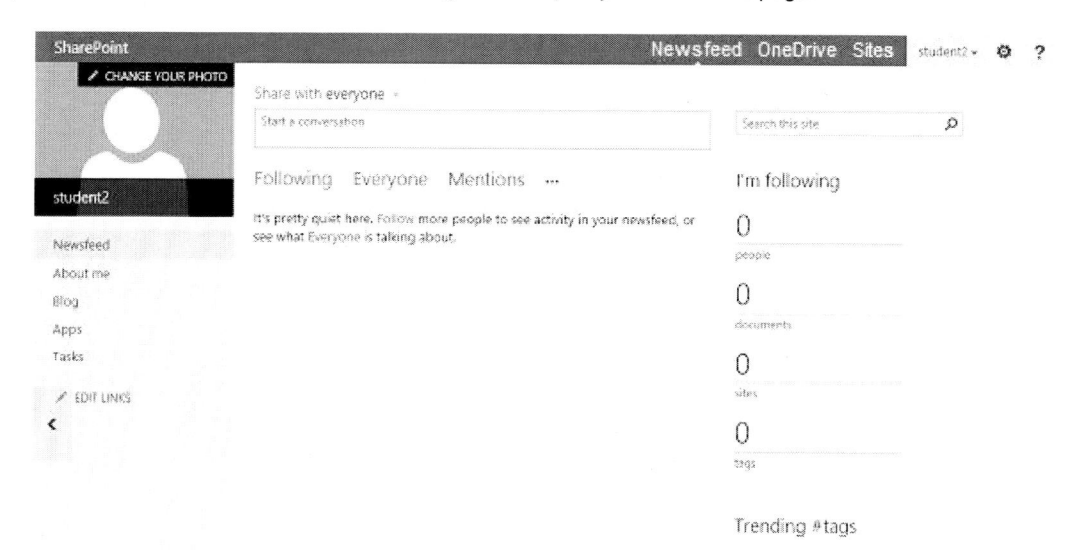

    b) If a dialog box is displayed with **Let's get social** selected, select **OK**.
    c) Review the content and options available in your Newsfeed.

    > **Note:** Your **Newsfeed**, **OneDrive**, and **Sites** will be largely empty at this stage. In a later lesson, you will add content and perform other tasks that will make updates appear here.

    d) Select the **back** button to return to the **Developer Team Site Home** page.

7. Access and create your OneDrive.

a) On the header, select **OneDrive** to configure and open your **OneDrive** page.

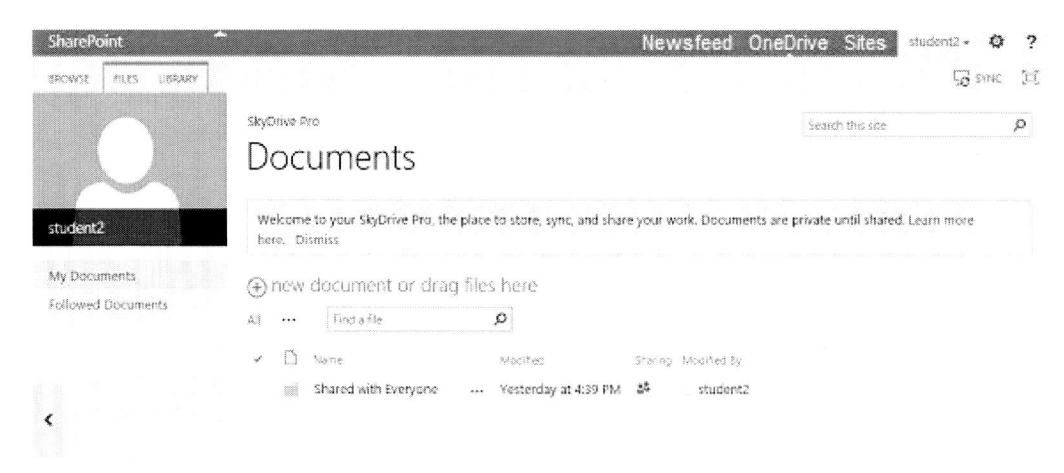

b) Review the content and options available in your OneDrive.
c) Select the **back** button to return to the **Developer Team Site Home** page.

8. Access and create your sites.
   a) On the header, select **Sites** to configure and open your **Sites** page.

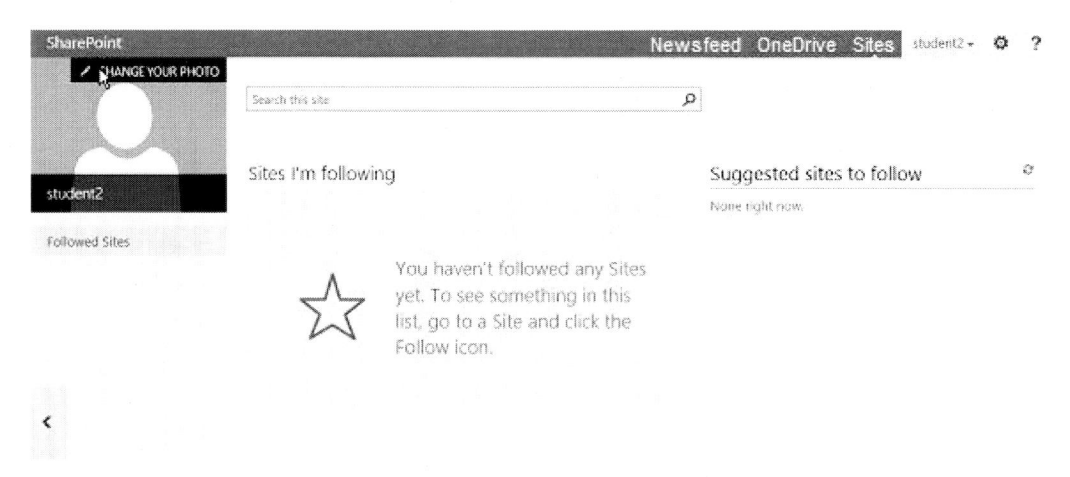

   b) Review the content and options available in your **Sites** page.

9. Review your account and **Settings** options.
   a) Select the **back** button to return to the **Developer Team Site** page.
   b) On the header, select your user name to make the name menu appear.
   c) Review the content and options available on the user name menu.

d) On the header, select the **Settings** button to make the **Settings** menu appear.

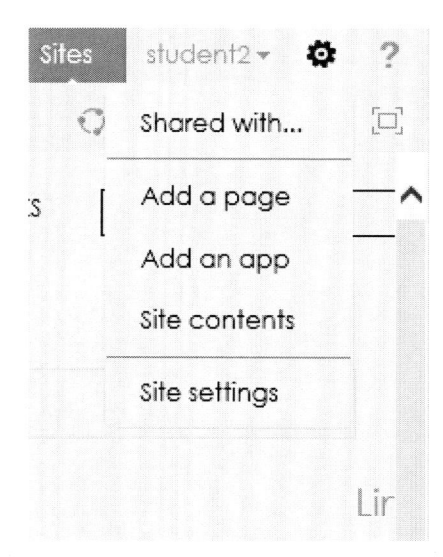

```
Sites   student2 ▼  ⚙  ?
            ↻  Shared with...   ⌑
    s   |       Add a page         ─ ∧
                Add an app
                Site contents
                ─────────────
                Site settings

                                Lir
```

e) Observe the options available on the **Settings** menu.

> **Note:** The options that are available on the **Settings** menu depend on the permissions that have been granted to your user account. Site owners and designers will have different options available compared to site members.

Summary

In this lesson, you learned about collaboration technologies, SharePoint versions, hierarchy, sites, groups, permissions levels, and interface elements. You accessed your SharePoint site and became familiar with it by navigating the site libraries, lists, and subsites.

How do you think you will use SharePoint in your organization?

In what ways would you like to use SharePoint in your organization that you're not currently?

> **Note:** Check your LogicalCHOICE Course screen for opportunities to interact with your classmates, peers, and the larger LogicalCHOICE online community about the topics covered in this course or other topics you are interested in. From the Course screen you can also access available resources for a more continuous learning experience.

2 | Working with Documents, Content, and Libraries

Lesson Time: 1 hour

Lesson Objectives

In this lesson, you will:

- Upload documents to SharePoint Libraries.
- Search for and preview documents in SharePoint libraries.

Lesson Introduction

In the previous lesson you accessed and took a tour of your SharePoint® team site. Now it's time to start using SharePoint. One of the primary functions of SharePoint is to provide a central place for people to share and collaborate on documents, spreadsheets, presentations, and other types of files. In SharePoint, documents and data are stored in libraries. Libraries are one of the most commonly used content structures in SharePoint. In this lesson, you will work with documents and content in libraries.

SharePoint is popular for document sharing and collaboration because it provides a central location for sharing documents rather than mapped network drives or local hard drives. By using SharePoint, the documents are stored centrally and are easily accessible to all members from their browsers or mobile devices. SharePoint also provides access control and management of the documents and data it stores, helping to ensure that only authorized people can access and make changes to files.

TOPIC A

Upload Documents

Opening, editing, and sharing documents are some of the most common ways people collaborate with SharePoint. Before you can edit or share documents, you first need to upload your documents to SharePoint. In this topic you will upload documents to SharePoint.

SharePoint Libraries

SharePoint libraries provide a central location to store and access files securely. A document library may contain a single type of file, such as documents or pictures, or multiple types of documents, such as spreadsheets and presentations. SharePoint also has features that allow users and administrators to manage the data stored in libraries. For example, documents can be added to a workflow to ensure forms and applications go through the appropriate approval process. Content can be uploaded and made available for sharing immediately or it can be held until approved. You can view document version histories and check files in and out of SharePoint, helping to ensure that you are working on the latest versions, and co-authoring documents effectively without having to worry about overwriting someone else's work. SharePoint also offers robust search and filtering capabilities to help you find the information you're looking for quickly. Libraries can be synchronized to your local computer for offline access. Site owners and designers may create any number of document libraries depending on how they wish to segregate the information stored on the site. The number and type of document libraries in a site, and the features enabled on those document libraries, are determined by the site owners and site designers, and may vary a great deal from site to site.

Library Folders

You can create folders in most libraries. You use these folders the same way you would within a file share, to organize and group your files rather than having them in one large list.

Ways to Add Documents to Libraries

There are many ways to add documents to a SharePoint library:

- Uploading using the **Add Document** option from SharePoint and browsing to the files you wish to upload.
- Dragging and dropping files from your desktop to the library.
- Creating a new document from the SharePoint menu using an installed application such as Microsoft® Office or Office Web Apps.
- Sending an email with an attachment to the library.

SharePoint Library Types

There are several types of SharePoint libraries that provide different functionality. The table below lists the types of libraries available in SharePoint.

Library Type	Purpose
Document	Allows you to store, organize, sync, and share documents, spreadsheets, and presentations. Any type of file can be uploaded to this type of library. New files created in this library are limited to a single type (i.e. Word, Excel®, PowerPoint®, etc.) chosen by the site owner.

Library Type	Purpose
Form	Allows you to store and manage business forms like status reports, purchase orders or other forms your organization may use. Forms libraries store form data in XML and provide more options for transforming and reusing the data. Form libraries require a compatible XML editor such as Microsoft® InfoPath®.
Wiki Page	A wiki page, like wiki websites, form an interconnected set of web pages that are easy to edit and contain text, images, and rich content, as well as SharePoint components. Wikis are a good way to collaboratively build and update content on selected topics. In some respects, wikis are like living documents that are constantly being updated and improved by everyone using the wiki.
Picture	Allows you to store and share pictures. This library is optimized for storing and displaying pictures and has slideshow capability.
Data Connection	Stores files that contain information about external data connections. For example, if you have a spreadsheet that collects information from multiple data sources such as an Access® database, a SQL Server database, and from an XML data source, you can use the Data Connection Library to create data connections that link the spreadsheet to the required data sources. The spreadsheet remains centrally stored and shared in SharePoint, and gets updated automatically from the connected data sources without the need to manually update it.
Report Library	Allows you to create and manage report and dashboard pages. These types of pages track metrics, goals, and business intelligence information. The reports and dashboards are Excel based.
Asset Library	Allows you to store and manage rich media assets such as image, audio, and video files. This library supports a variety of media content.

> **Note:** To learn more about SharePoint Wiki Page libraries, refer to the LearnTO **Use and Edit a Wiki Page** presentation from the **LearnTO** tile on the LogicalCHOICE Course screen.

Microsoft Office Web Apps

Microsoft Office Web Apps are online versions of Microsoft Word, Excel, PowerPoint, and OneNote that are designed to allow users to view and edit Office documents from anywhere using a web browser. Office Web Apps are considered companion versions to Office applications and are not as fully featured. Office Web Apps integrate with Microsoft SharePoint, providing enhanced features for document libraries, including the ability to view, share, and edit documents from PCs, tablets, and smartphones over the web.

Requirements for Office Web Apps

To use Office Web Apps, a supported version of Internet Explorer®, Firefox®, or Safari® is required. Some mobile functionality may require Office Mobile 2010 or 2013.

Availability of Office Web Apps

Office Web Apps is available through Windows Live® to consumers and small-business users and is offered as a free service. Business customers who meet Microsoft Office licensing requirements may deploy Office Web Apps servers or farms to integrate with SharePoint or other applications. You can download Office Web Apps from the Microsoft Download Center.

> **Note:** For additional information on planning for Office Web Apps, requirements, and availability see the following link: **http://technet.microsoft.com/en-us/library/ff431682.aspx.**

SharePoint Integration with Office Web Apps

Office Web Apps integrates with SharePoint to provide enhanced options for document creation and preview, as well as cross-platform support for collaboration using the online versions of Office tools. After you integrate Office Web Apps with SharePoint, Office Web Apps displays different menus in SharePoint document libraries, allowing you to choose and create a Word, Excel, PowerPoint or OneNote document. A non-integrated SharePoint server is limited to creating a single type of document (Word, or Excel, or PowerPoint, or OneNote). Office Web Apps also provides a preview window allowing you to see the document, spreadsheet, presentation, or notebook you have selected. This can be helpful when comparing versions of documents, or when you need to identify a document by its content rather than its file name. Office Web Apps also allows users on PC, Mac®, and other platforms to create, view, and collaborate with the same productivity software, provided each type of platform has a compatible browser. Finally, Office Web Apps allows you to remotely collaborate while away from your desktop by using an Internet kiosk, tablet, or smartphone and a compatible browser.

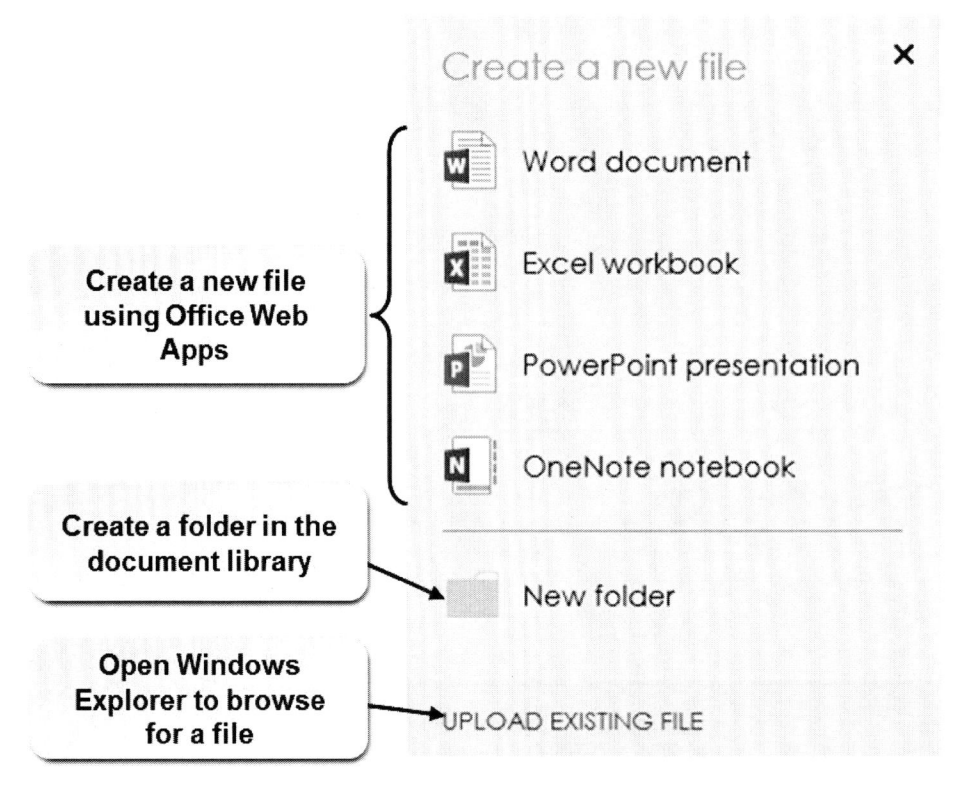

Figure 2-1: The Office Web Apps document creation menu.

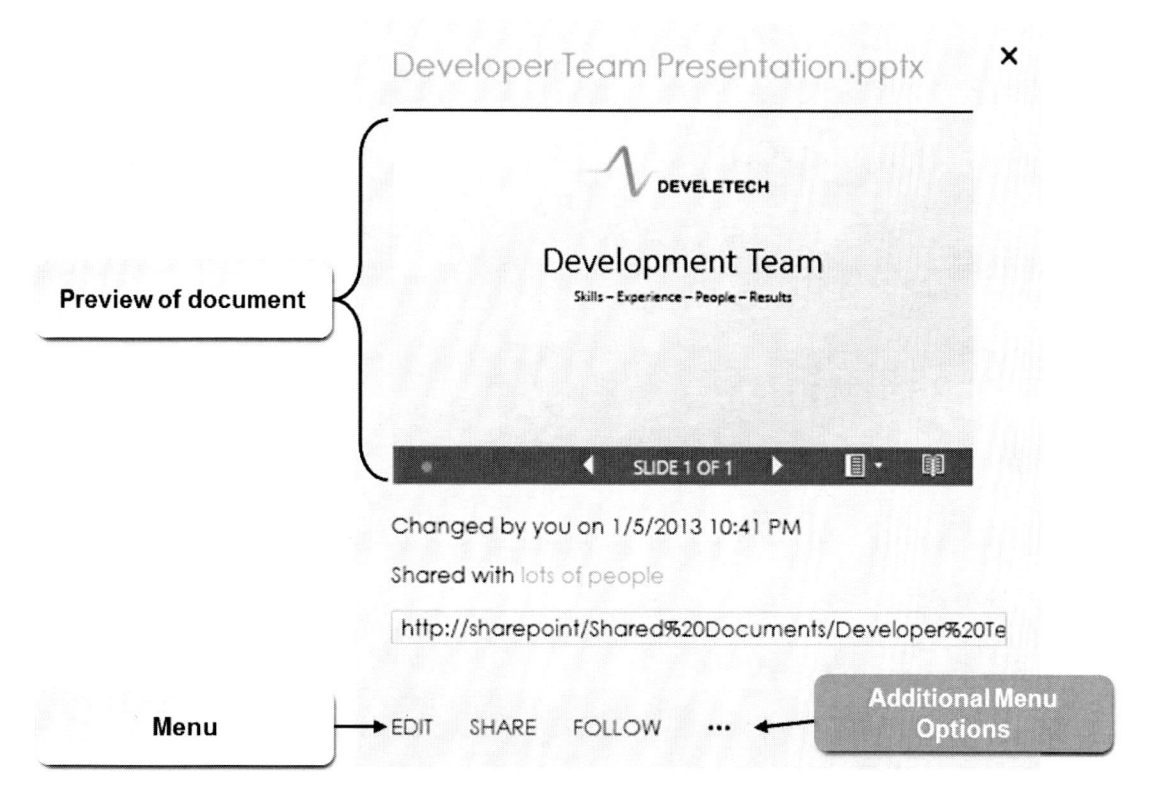

Figure 2-2: The Office Web Apps preview window.

	Access the Checklist tile on your CHOICE Course screen for reference information and job aids on How to Upload Documents.

ACTIVITY 2-1
Uploading Documents

Data Files
C:\091107Data\Working With Documents, Content, and Libraries\Resume.docx

C:\091107Data\Working With Documents, Content, and Libraries\Work Skills Matrix.xlsx

C:\091107Data\Working With Documents, Content, and Libraries\Resume and Work Skills Presentation.pptx

C:\091107Data\Working With Documents, Content, and Libraries\Project Orange Specification Addendum.docx

C:\091107Data\Working With Documents, Content, and Libraries\Empty.docx

Before You Begin
You should be logged onto the classroom SharePoint site, and your browser should have the Developer Team Site page open.

Scenario
Now that you are familiar with the Develetech Developer Team site, you need to add some personal information and a skills matrix to the Team Document library, as well as some project specific documents to the Project Orange, Orange Documents library. You have some existing documents that you will upload to the sites, and you will create a new document from the site as well.

---

1. Upload a file from SharePoint.
   a) In the **Quick Launch** area, select **Team Documents** to open the Team Documents document library.
   b) Review the documents in the Team Documents document library.

Team Documents

⊕ new document or drag files here

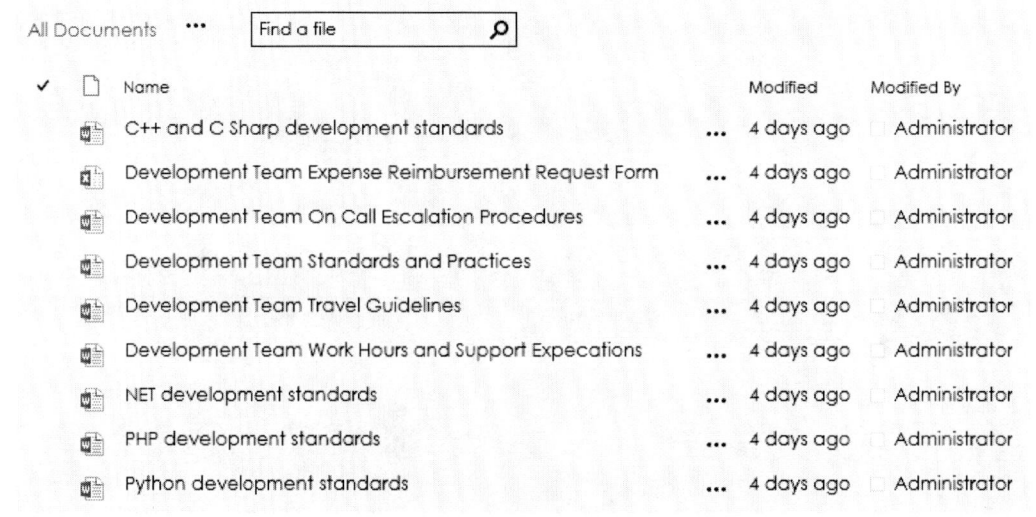

All Documents ···   Find a file

✓	☐	Name		Modified	Modified By
		C++ and C Sharp development standards	···	4 days ago	Administrator
		Development Team Expense Reimbursement Request Form	···	4 days ago	Administrator
		Development Team On Call Escalation Procedures	···	4 days ago	Administrator
		Development Team Standards and Practices	···	4 days ago	Administrator
		Development Team Travel Guidelines	···	4 days ago	Administrator
		Development Team Work Hours and Support Expecations	···	4 days ago	Administrator
		NET development standards	···	4 days ago	Administrator
		PHP development standards	···	4 days ago	Administrator
		Python development standards	···	4 days ago	Administrator

c) Select **new document**. The **Create a new file** context menu appears.

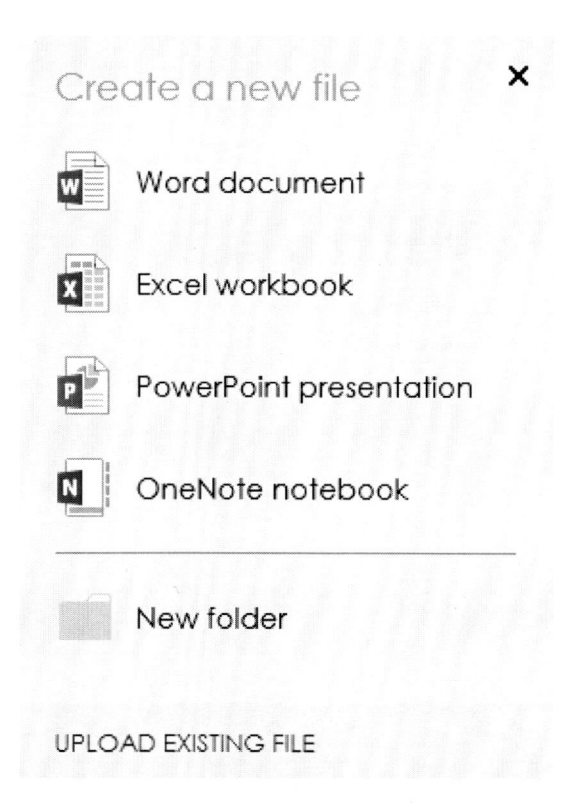

    Create a new file   ✕

    - Word document
    - Excel workbook
    - PowerPoint presentation
    - OneNote notebook
    - New folder

    UPLOAD EXISTING FILE

d) Observe the options available on the **Create a new file** menu.
e) Select **UPLOAD EXISTING FILE**.
f) In the **Add a document** dialog box, select **Browse**.

> **Note:** You can also use the **FILES** tab on the ribbon to upload files.

g) In the **Choose File to Upload** dialog box, navigate to and open the **C:\091107Data\Working With Documents, Content, and Libraries** folder.

h) Rename the **Resume** document to *<Your User Name> Resume*

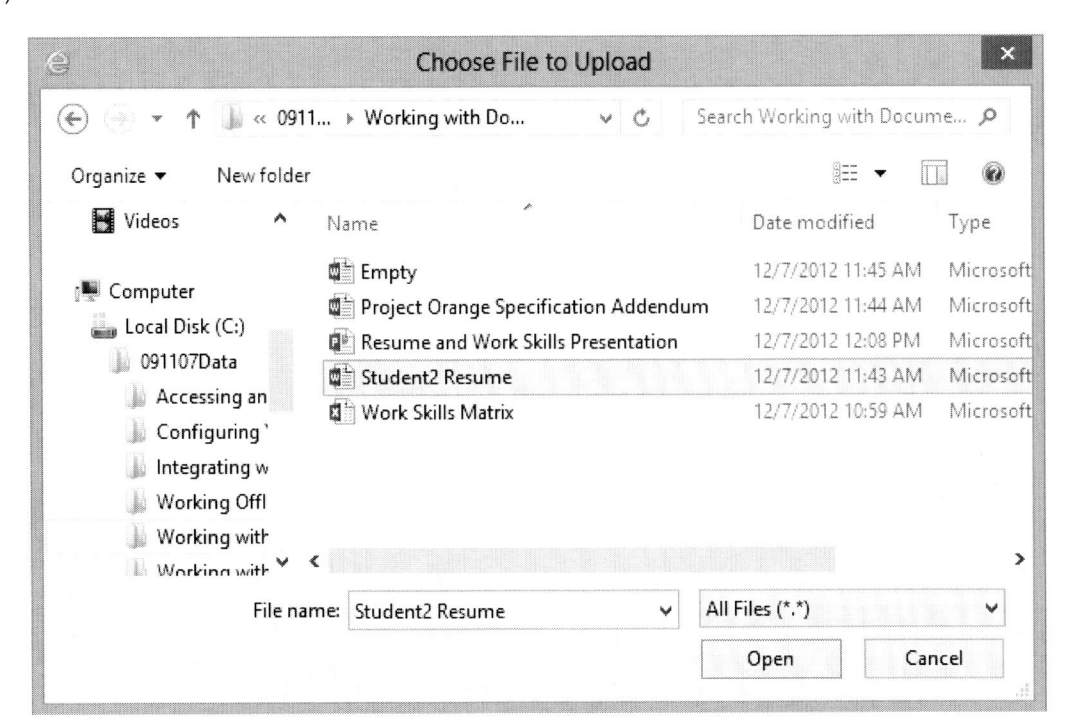

> **Note:** To rename a document in Windows Explorer, right-click on the document and select **Rename** from the shortcut menu.

i) Select **<your user name> Resume** and select **Open**.
j) Select **OK**.

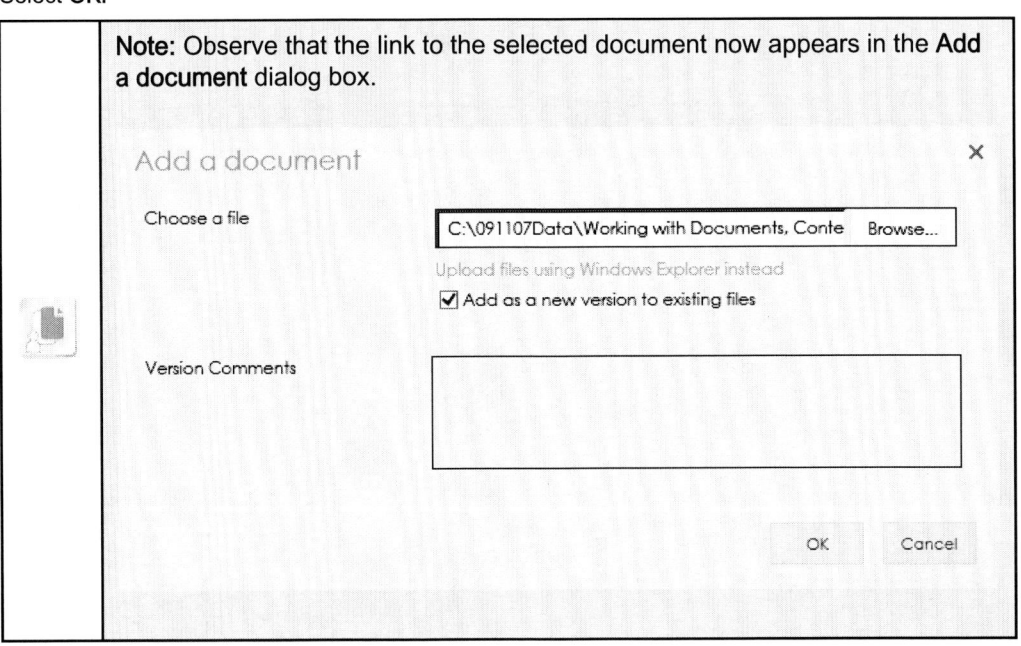

> **Note:** Observe that the link to the selected document now appears in the **Add a document** dialog box.

k) Observe the file in the document library.

Team Documents ⓘ

⊕ new document or drag files here

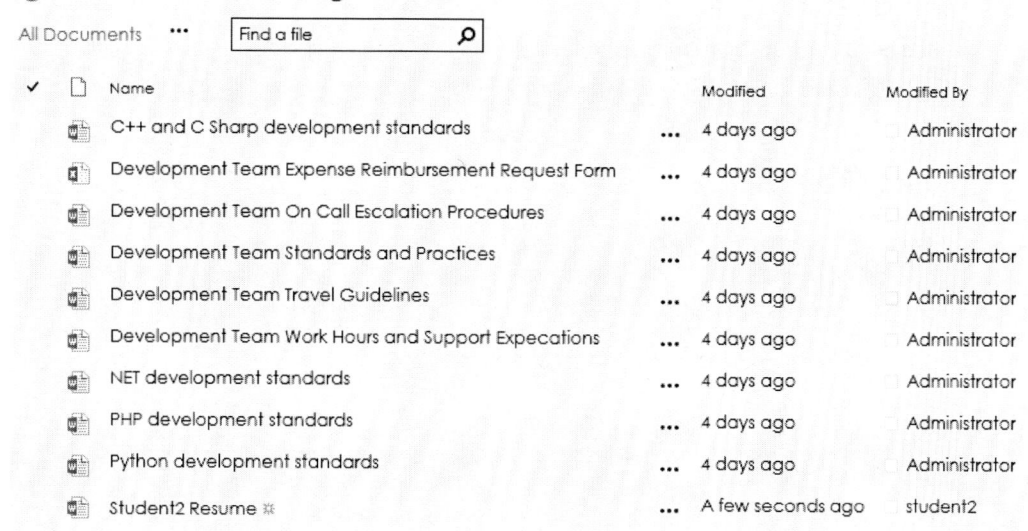

All Documents ···   [Find a file 🔍]

✓	Name		Modified	Modified By
	C++ and C Sharp development standards	···	4 days ago	Administrator
	Development Team Expense Reimbursement Request Form	···	4 days ago	Administrator
	Development Team On Call Escalation Procedures	···	4 days ago	Administrator
	Development Team Standards and Practices	···	4 days ago	Administrator
	Development Team Travel Guidelines	···	4 days ago	Administrator
	Development Team Work Hours and Support Expecations	···	4 days ago	Administrator
	NET development standards	···	4 days ago	Administrator
	PHP development standards	···	4 days ago	Administrator
	Python development standards	···	4 days ago	Administrator
	Student2 Resume ※	···	A few seconds ago	student2

2. Drag and drop files to SharePoint from Windows Explorer.
   a) If your browser is running in full screen mode, select the window control to switch to window mode.
   b) Open **Windows Explorer**.
   c) Navigate to **C:\091107Data\Working With Documents, Content, and Libraries**.
   d) Rename the spreadsheet **Work Skills Matrix** to *<Your User Name> Work Skills Matrix*
   e) Rename the presentation **Resume and Work Skills Presentation** to *<your user name> Resume and Work Skills Presentation*
   f) Select both the **<Your User Name> Work Skills Matrix** and **<Your User Name> Resume and Work Skills Presentation** files.

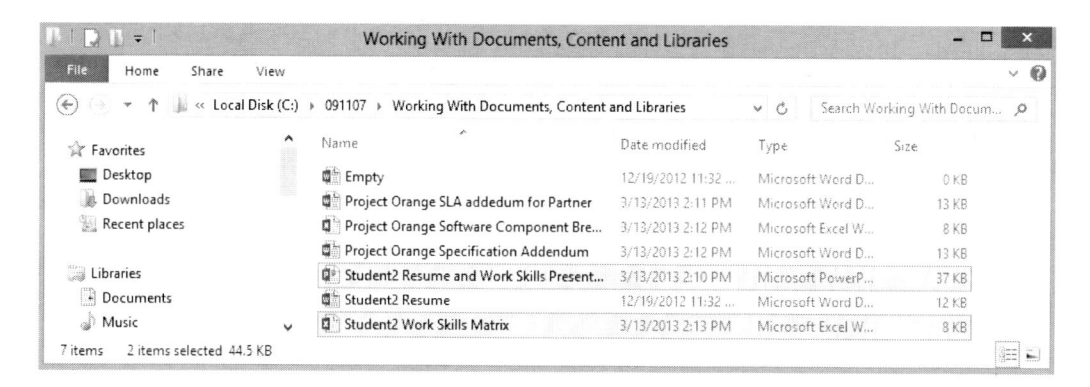

   g) Drag and drop the files from Windows Explorer onto the **Team Documents** document library in the browser window.

   > **Note:** You may need to reposition the two windows so that you can drag the two documents from Windows Explorer to the Team Documents document library properly.

   > **Note:** The **Drop here** box should appear when the two documents are dragged over the Team Documents area.

h) Maximize the browser window and observe the two files in the document library.

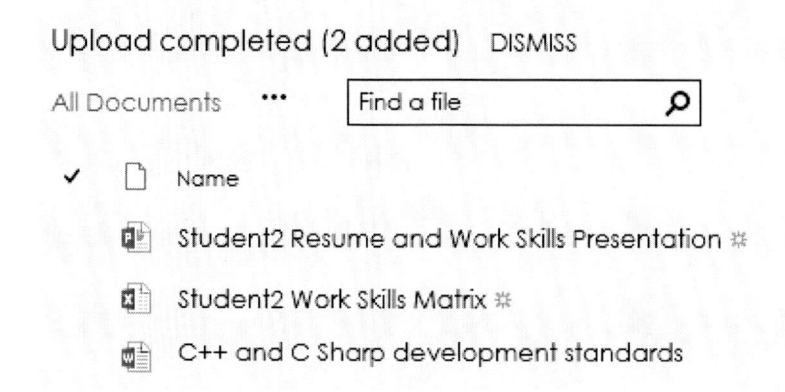

Team Documents

Upload completed (2 added)   DISMISS

All Documents •••   Find a file

✓   Name

- Student2 Resume and Work Skills Presentation
- Student2 Work Skills Matrix
- C++ and C Sharp development standards

3. Upload files to the Project Orange site.
   a) In the **Quick Launch** area of the SharePoint site, under **Subsites**, select **Project Orange**. The Project Orange team site appears.
   b) If needed, scroll the browser window so that you can see the **Orange Documents** document library.

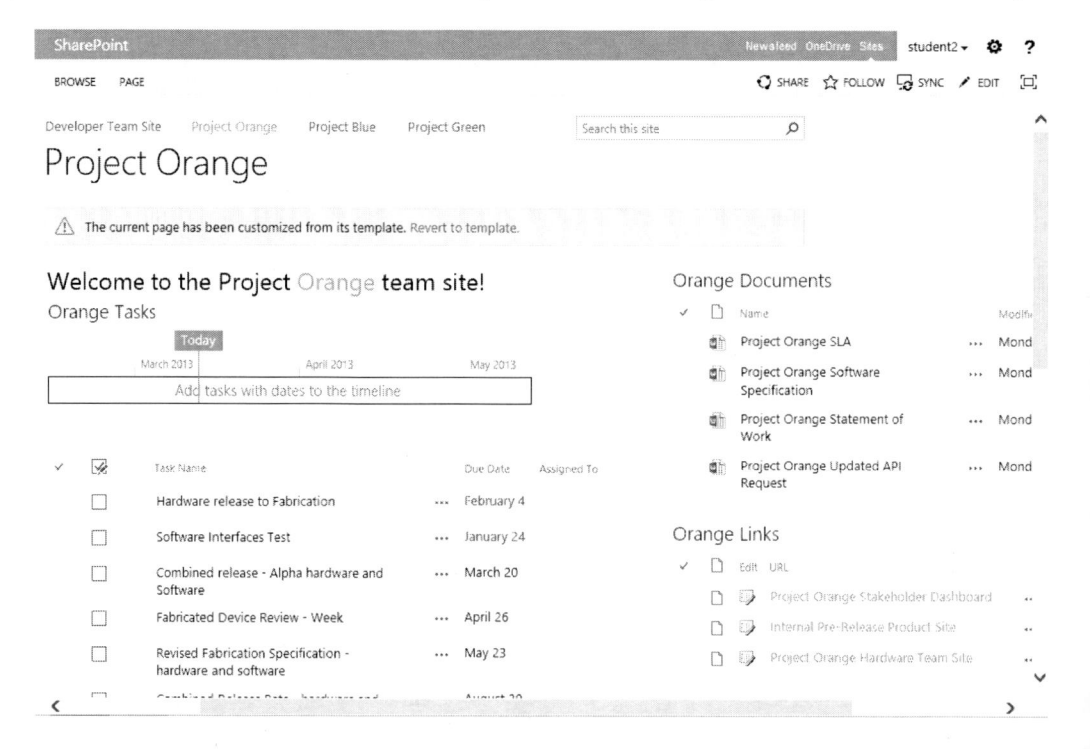

   c) Switch to Windows Explorer. Rename the file **Project Orange Specification Addendum** to *<Your User Name> Project Orange Specification Addendum*.
   d) Drag and drop **<Your User Name> Project Orange Specification Addendum** into the **Orange Documents** document library.

e) Switch to the browser and observe the new file in the **Orange Documents** document library. See the green arrow attached to the document icon showing that the document is checked out.

Orange Documents

Upload completed with 1 checked out (1 added)   DISMISS

✓	☐	Name		Modified	Modified By
	📄	Student2 Project Orange Specification Addendum	...	A few seconds ago	student2
	📄	Project Orange SLA	...	Monday at 4:28 PM	Administrator
	📄	Project Orange Software Specification	...	Monday at 4:28 PM	Administrator
	📄	Project Orange Statement of Work	...	Monday at 4:28 PM	Administrator
	📄	Project Orange Updated API Request	...	Monday at 4:28 PM	Administrator

   f) Select **Orange Documents** to open the document library.

4. Create a new document.
   a) Select **new document**, and then select **Word document**.
   b) In the **Create a new document** dialog box, in the **Document Name** box, type *<Your User Name> test cases* and select **OK**. The Microsoft Office Web Apps version of Word opens with a blank document.
   c) In the document, type *<Your User Name> test cases*
   d) On the **Quick Access** toolbar, select **Save**.
   e) In the Ribbon, select **OPEN IN WORD**.
   f) In **Microsoft Word**, select **FILE,** and then select **Info**.
   g) Select **Check In**.

   > **Note:** You will learn more about checking documents in later in this course.

   h) In the **Check In** dialog box, under **Version Type,** select **1.0 Major Version (publish),** and then select **OK**.
   i) Close **Microsoft Word**.
   j) In the **We're opening your document in Microsoft Word** dialog box, select **My document opened successfully, close Word Web App**.

   > **Note:** When you close the document you will be automatically taken back to the **Orange Documents** document library page.

   k) Observe the new document in the document library.

5. Upload an empty file to see SharePoint's interaction with empty files.
   a) Select **new document** and then select **UPLOAD EXISTING FILE**.
   b) In the **Add a document** dialog box, select **Browse**.
   c) In the **Choose File to Upload** dialog box, select **Empty** and then select **Open**.

   > **Note:** The dialog box should already be at the C:\091107Data\Working with Documents Content and Libraries\ folder. If not, navigate to that location.

   d) In the **Add a document** dialog box, select **OK**.
   e) Select **Cancel**.

f) Switch to Windows Explorer.
g) Drag and drop **Empty** to the **Orange Documents** document library.
h) Switch back to your browser.
i) In SharePoint, select **All Documents** in order to refresh the page and clear the error message display.
j) In the **Top Links** bar, select **Developer Team Site**.

TOPIC B

Search for Documents and Files

By uploading your first documents to SharePoint, you are already taking advantage of the core SharePoint capabilities of centralized storage, and secured access. To get the most out of SharePoint, you can edit document properties to better describe your document. You can provide keywords so that it is indexed properly and others can find the document easily using keyword searches, and when creating filtered lists. By populating document properties effectively and utilizing SharePoint's search features, you can find what you're looking for faster, and help ensure that others can find the information that you're sharing.

Enterprise Keywords

Keywords are words or phrases that people use to search for information on search engines, websites, and in SharePoint. A keyword or key phrase might be something like "travel" or "expense" that will allow you to find documents and other information related to the terms that you are searching for. SharePoint has a feature called *Enterprise Keywords* that can be enabled by site owners. This provides a database called the Managed Team Store where it stores keywords that are associated with documents and other information. Users can associate keywords with documents to allow other users to find those documents when the keywords are searched for. For example, the HR department might tag the Travel Expense Guidelines document with the keywords "travel" and "expense" to make sure that document is found when either of those terms are searched for.

SharePoint Search

SharePoint provides text based search boxes on sites, pages, lists, and libraries. Like most other web-based search interfaces, in SharePoint, users can type keywords into the search box, select the search button and get a list of items that match the criteria typed in the search box. SharePoint search should provide a quick and easy way to narrow the list of documents and items displayed, and help you find the specific documents you want.

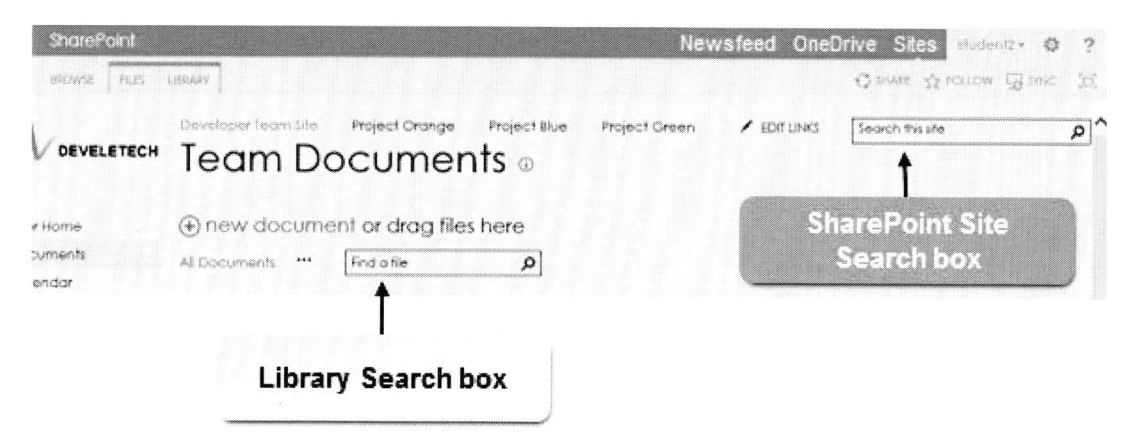

Figure 2-3: SharePoint search boxes.

Factors Impacting SharePoint Search

The results displayed from a search depend on many factors including the context of the search. For example, a search run on the site will search the entire site, while a search run in a document library will search only that library. Other factors that impact search results include whether the Enterprise

Keyword feature has been enabled, if documents have been tagged with keywords, and the frequency with which SharePoint updates its index.

Document Properties

> **Note:** Enterprise Keywords are not enabled by default in SharePoint libraries. If you don't see the Enterprise Keywords field when looking at document or item properties, then Enterprise Keywords have not been enabled for the library or list.

SharePoint stores information about documents so that documents can be more easily organized and found through searches. By default, the only two properties available are Name and Title. Site owners can add more properties to describe documents. It is common for site owners to enable the Enterprise Keywords feature in SharePoint to allow for site searches based on keywords. When Enterprise Keywords is enabled for a library, the Enterprise Keywords property becomes available as well. The following table briefly describes these properties.

Property	Description
Name	This is the file name of the document in question.
Title	This is the descriptive title for the document. This can be different from the file name, and is usually more descriptive. The title is what appears in the list of documents when viewing items in a document library.
Enterprise Keywords	Terms that you tag a document with by entering them in the Enterprise Keyword property box. Multiple keywords can be associated, and each keyword or keyword set must be separated by a semicolon. When entering keywords, a list of similar keywords from the Managed Term Store will appear in a drop-down box. Examples of keywords that might be stored as properties for a document could be a project name associated with a document, a related technology, an organizational department, or business circumstance the document applies to.

Document Properties and Site Owners

Site owners may add other properties to describe documents. For example, a site owner may add a project name property, to categorize documents based on their project or they may add department properties to allow documents to be categorized that way.

SharePoint Alerts

An alert allows SharePoint to notify you if specific events take place in the SharePoint site. For document libraries, you can be notified if the library or specific documents are updated. For lists, you can receive notifications if new items are added, or if existing items are modified or deleted. Alerts are configured by you and can be sent through e-mail or via text message. You can choose what triggers the alert and when you are notified, as well as configure the alert to notify multiple people.

Alert Examples

There are many reasons to set up alerts for SharePoint lists, libraries, documents, and items. If you are managing a project and waiting for documentation to be posted to a document library for the project, you might set up an alert so that you will be notified when anything changes in the library. If you have created a document that is shared with your colleagues, you may set an alert so that you are notified whenever that document is changed. If you are managing a team, you may wish to get a daily notification when new items are added to the team calendar.

Available Alerts

The alerts that are available on your SharePoint site depend on how site owners have set up and configured the SharePoint server or farm. Outbound email must be configured for email alerts, and outbound text messaging must be configured for text alerts to be available.

> **Access the Checklist tile on your CHOICE Course screen for reference information and job aids on How to Modify Document Properties and Search for Documents.**

ACTIVITY 2-2
Modifying Document Properties and Searching for Documents

Before You Begin
You should be logged into the classroom SharePoint site and your browser should have the Developer Team Site page open.

Scenario
Now that you know how to add files to the Develetech Developer Team site, you need to know how to search for documents which you need to view, edit, and share. You will view and edit the properties of some documents in the Team Documents document library and ensure that they have keywords and titles that are appropriate when searching for them. You will then perform some searches to verify that the results are working as expected and set an alert. You will share a document in the Team Documents document library and download it to ensure it is working as intended. Finally, you will review the **FILES** ribbon commands to become more familiar with them and review email messages from SharePoint to verify the alerts you set are working as expected.

1. View document properties and keywords.
    a) In the **Quick Launch** area, select **Team Documents**.
    b) In the **Team Documents** page, next to the **C++ and C Sharp development standards** document, select the **Open Menu** ••• button. The preview window will open.
    c) Observe the menu options at the bottom of the preview window. Select the **Open Menu** ••• button in the preview window.

d) Select **View Properties**. The document properties are displayed on the page.

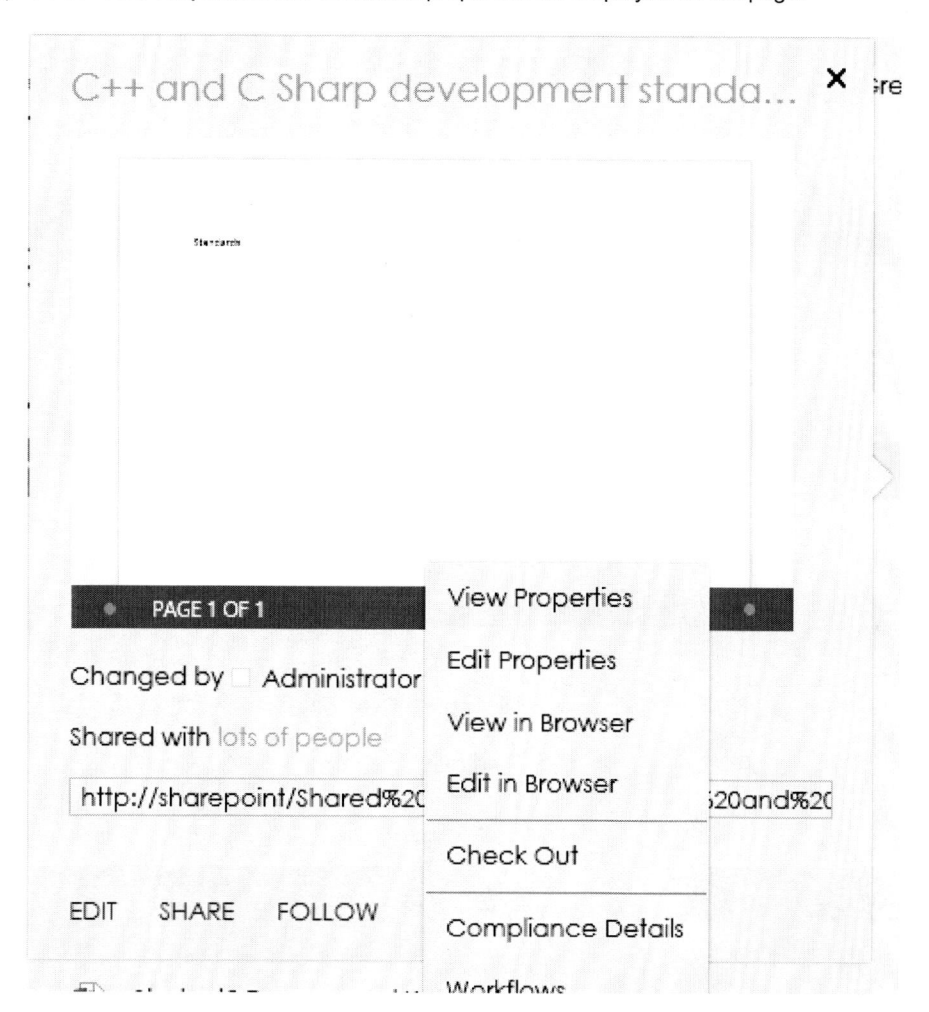

e) Observe the document properties and keywords that are associated with this document.
f) Select **Close**.

2. Update document properties for your résumé.
    a) If necessary, navigate to **Team Documents**.
    b) Next to **<Your Student Name> Resume**, select the **Open Menu** button.

c) In the preview window, select the **Open Menu** button, and then select **Edit Properties**.

d) The document properties are displayed on the page. In the **Title** box, verify *<Your Student Name> Resume* is displayed.

e) In the **Enterprise Keywords** box, type *<Your Student Name>; Resume*

> **Note:** Be sure to separate your keywords with a semicolon.

f) Select **Save**.

3. Update document properties for your résumé and résumé work skills document.
    a) Next to *<Your Student Name> Resume and Work Skills Presentation*, select the **Open Menu** button.
    b) In the preview window, select the **Open Menu** button, and then select **Edit Properties**.
    c) The document properties are displayed on the page. In the **Title** box, type *<Your Student Name> Resume and Work Skills*
    d) In the **Enterprise Keywords** box, type *<Your Student Name>; Resume; Skills*

> **Note:** As you enter keywords in the **Enterprise Keywords** box, keywords that have previously been entered will appear in the drop-down box. This includes keywords typed by classmates.

    e) Select **Save**.

4. Update document properties for your work skills matrix.
    a) Next to *<Your Student Name> Work Skills Matrix*, select the **Open Menu** button.

b) In the preview window, select the **Open Menu** button, and then select **Edit Properties**.
c) The document properties are displayed on the page. In the **Title** box, verify *<Your Student Name> Work Skills Matrix* is displayed.
d) In the **Enterprise Keywords** box, type *<Your Student Name>; Skills*
e) Select **Save**.

5. Search for documents using Site Search.
   a) In the upper-right corner of the page, in the **Search this site** box, type *standards* and select the **Search** button.

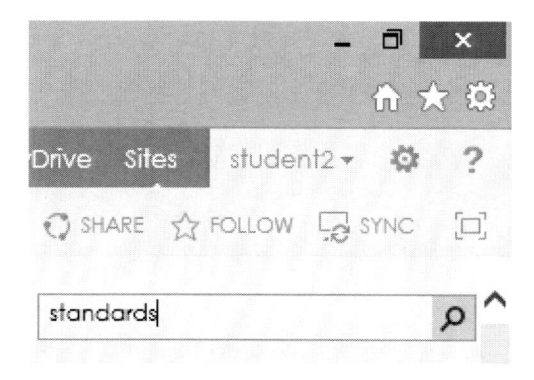

   b) In the **Search** page, the results are displayed.
   c) Observe the search results.

   > **Note:** Because the search was executed from the Site Search box, the search not only returns documents that contain the term being searched for, but also any libraries and lists that contain the term, or documents with the term. In this case, the Team Documents library is listed because it contains the documents with the term searched for.

6. Set an alert to inform you when changes are made to documents.
   a) At the bottom of the **Search** page, select **Alert Me** to display the **New Alert** page.
   b) Observe the Alert Title and the Delivery Method that are chosen by default.
   c) In **Delivery Method** section, verify that the email address is *<Your User Name>@develetech.com*.
   d) In the **Change Type** section, observe the types of actions that can generate an alert, then select **All changes**.

e) In the **When to Send Alerts** section, observe the options, then verify **Send a daily summary** is selected.

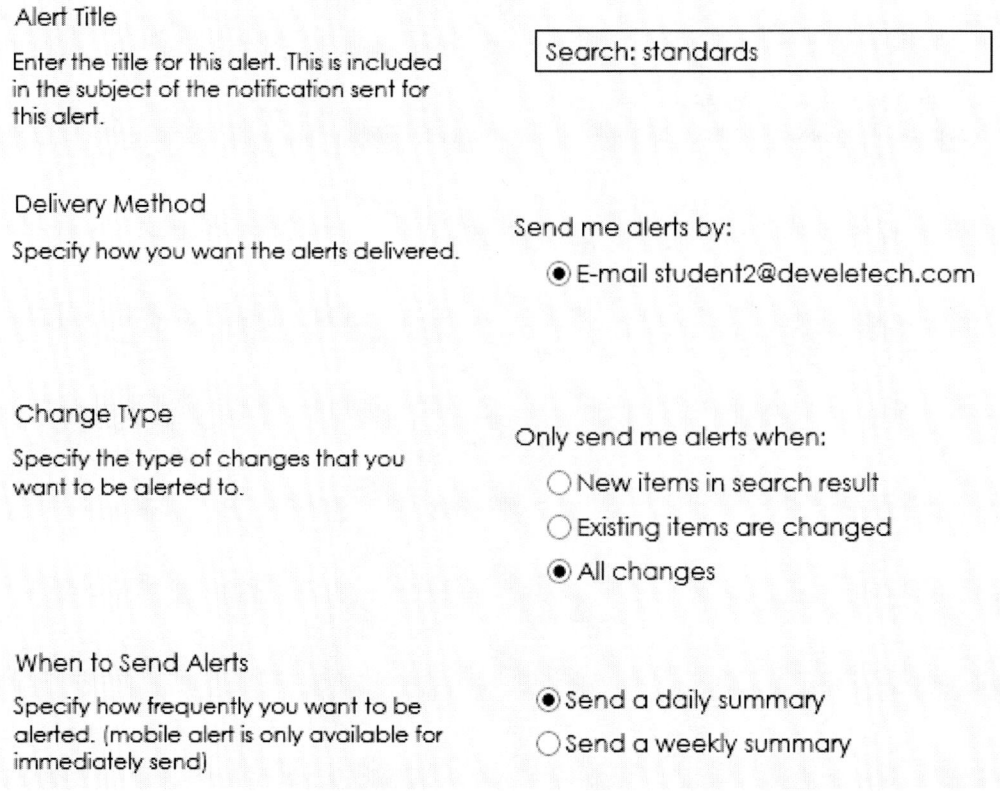

```
Alert Title                                          Search: standards
Enter the title for this alert. This is included
in the subject of the notification sent for
this alert.

Delivery Method                                      Send me alerts by:
Specify how you want the alerts delivered.
                                                     ● E-mail student2@develetech.com

Change Type                                          Only send me alerts when:
Specify the type of changes that you                 ○ New items in search result
want to be alerted to.                               ○ Existing items are changed
                                                     ● All changes

When to Send Alerts                                  ● Send a daily summary
Specify how frequently you want to be                ○ Send a weekly summary
alerted. (mobile alert is only available for
immediately send)
```

f) Select **OK**.
g) On the **Search** page, point to the first document in the list. The document preview will appear.
h) Under the document preview, select **VIEW LIBRARY** to switch to the The Team Documents library.

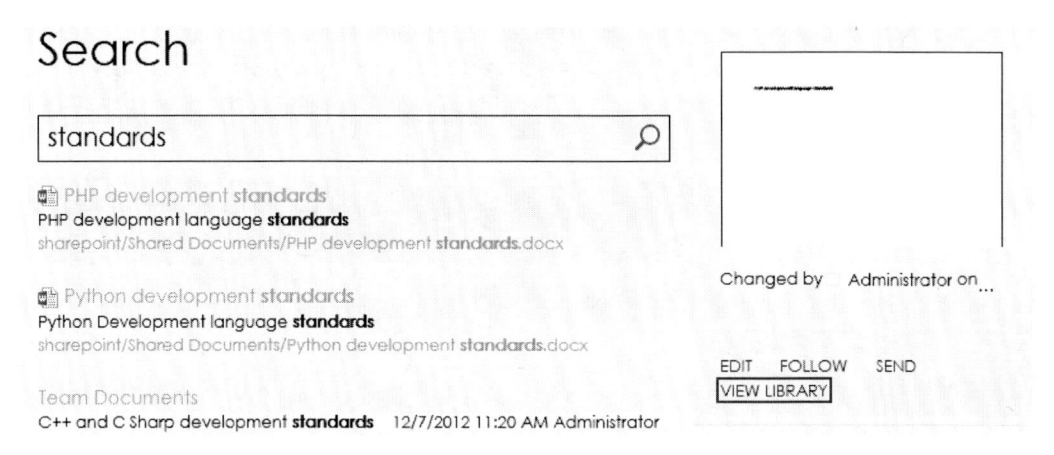

```
Search

[ standards                                    🔍 ]

📄 PHP development standards
PHP development language standards
sharepoint/Shared Documents/PHP development standards.docx

📄 Python development standards
Python Development language standards
sharepoint/Shared Documents/Python development standards.docx

Team Documents
C++ and C Sharp development standards   12/7/2012 11:20 AM Administrator
```

Changed by   Administrator on...

EDIT   FOLLOW   SEND
VIEW LIBRARY

7. Observe the difference in search results when performing a site search compared to a search of a specific document library.

a) In the **Find a file** box, type *standards* and select the **Search** button.

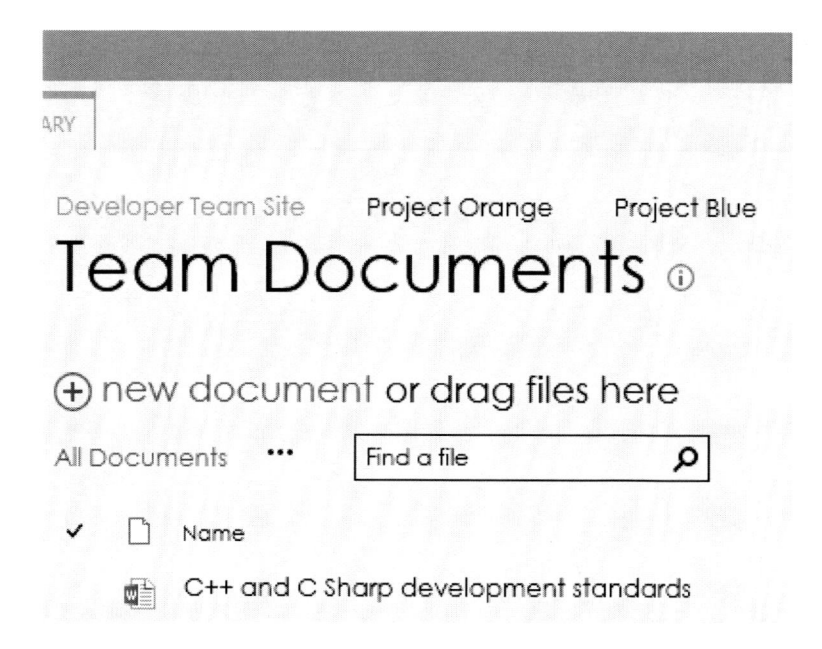

> Developer Team Site   Project Orange   Project Blue
>
> # Team Documents ⓘ
>
> ⊕ new document or drag files here
>
> All Documents •••   Find a file 🔍
>
> ✓ ☐ Name
>
>   📄 C++ and C Sharp development standards

b) Observe the list of files that appears.

> **Note:** Because you searched from the **Find a file** box inside the Team Documents library, the search scope is limited to only that library. The Team Documents library does not appear on the search results list.

8. Share a document
   a) In the **Team Documents** library, next to the **C++ and C Sharp development standards** document, select the **Open Menu** button.
   b) In the preview window, select **Share**.
   c) In the **Share** dialog box, in the **Enter names, email addresses, or Everyone** box, type *<Your User Name>* and select **Share**.
   d) Observe the message that appears in the upper right portion of the page.

   > **Note:** The message said, "Sharing request sent to site owner." A site owner has to approve the request to share the library.

9. Download a document.
   a) Next to the **C++ and C Sharp development standards** document, select the **Open Menu** button.
   b) In the preview window, select the **Open Menu** button, and then select **Download a copy**.
   c) A prompt appears at the bottom of the browser window, select **Save**. The save will complete.
   d) Select **View downloads**.

e) In the **View Downloads** window, select **Open**.

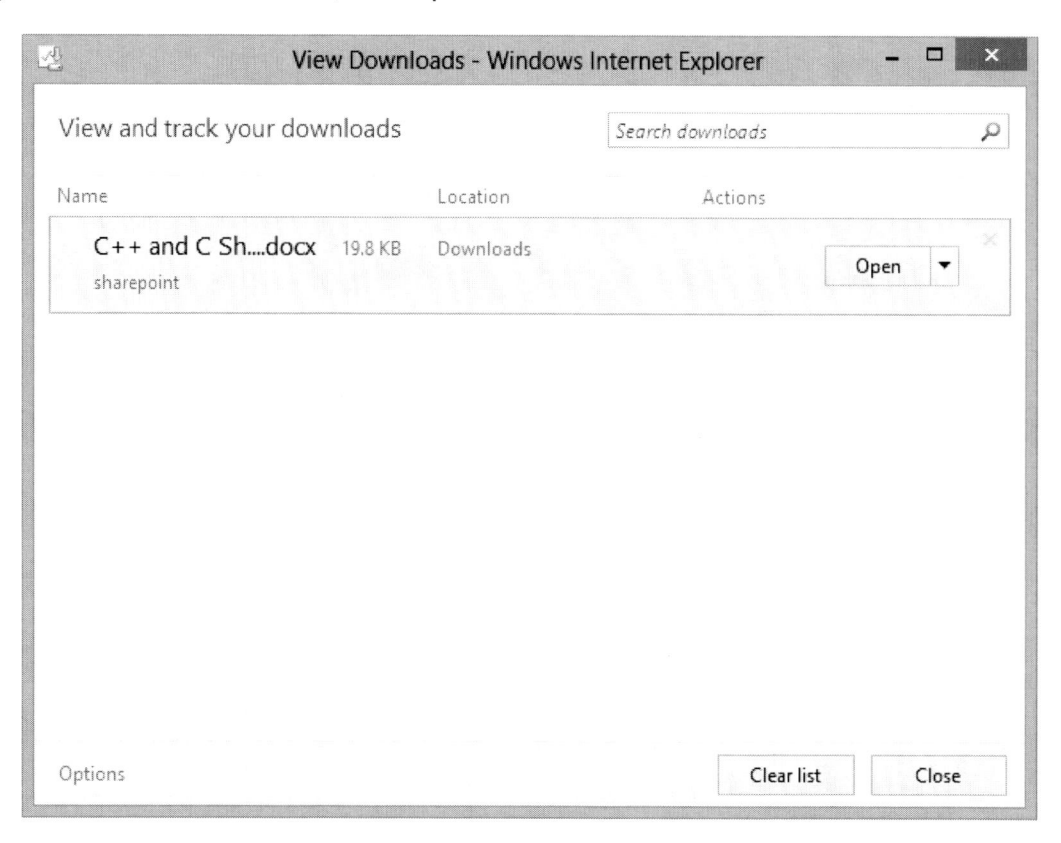

f) The document opens in Microsoft Word. Close **Microsoft Word**.
g) Select **Close** to close the **View Downloads** window.

10. Review ribbon commands
    a) On the ribbon, select the **FILES** tab. The **FILES** menu appears.

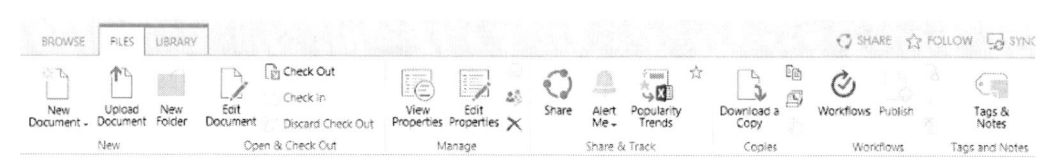

    b) Observe the button groups and actions available on the ribbon.

11. Review email for messages from SharePoint.
    a) Minimize your web browser.
    b) Open **Microsoft Outlook**. Your mailbox appears.
    c) If you receive a certificate error, select **Yes**.
    d) Observe the message you received from the Developer Team Site in your Inbox.
    e) Close **Microsoft Outlook.**
    f) Switch to your browser and select **Developer Team Site** to return to the **Developer Team Site** home page.

Summary

In this lesson, you learned about SharePoint libraries, the different types of libraries available in SharePoint, and how Office Web Apps integrate with SharePoint libraries. You uploaded documents to SharePoint using the web interface and Windows Explorer. You then learned how document properties and Enterprise Keywords are used in searches and about SharePoint alerts. You then updated the properties for several documents, performed searches for keywords, set and triggered alerts, and verified that the alerts were received.

How do you currently work with documents in your organization (how are they stored and how do people collaborate with them)?

How could SharePoint improve the way you work with and share documents in your organization?

> **Note:** Check your LogicalCHOICE Course screen for opportunities to interact with your classmates, peers, and the larger LogicalCHOICE online community about the topics covered in this course or other topics you are interested in. From the Course screen you can also access available resources for a more continuous learning experience.

3 | Working with Lists

Lesson Time: 1 hour, 15 minutes

Lesson Objectives

In this lesson, you will:

- Describe lists, types of lists and columns, and add list items.
- Modify list items.
- Create and modify list views.
- Filter and group list views based on criteria you select.

Lesson Introduction

Now that you know how to share and collaborate on files with document libraries, it's time to learn about lists. Lists are another commonly used content structure in SharePoint®. In this lesson, you will work with lists, list items, and list views.

Lists allow you to store different types of data that are useful when collaborating in teams and on projects such as calendar, task, or contact information. To get the most out of SharePoint you should understand how to use lists, the variety of lists that are available, and how to modify and customize list features.

TOPIC A

Add List Items

To start working with lists you need to know how lists are different from document libraries, and the types of lists that are available in SharePoint. In this topic, you will learn that fundamental information, and then you will perform one of the most common tasks in SharePoint, adding items to lists.

SharePoint Lists

SharePoint lists organize, store, and track information about a group of similar items. Unlike libraries which organize, store, and track documents which contain the information, a SharePoint list actually contains the information. For example, a contact list stores contact information such as name, address, and phone number. That information is entered into the contact list through a form provided by SharePoint and the data is stored in the SharePoint database. SharePoint provides built-in lists for communication, such as announcements and discussion boards, and lists for tracking information such as calendars, tasks, and links. You can also create custom lists that have exactly the columns that you wish to include.

List Variety in SharePoint Sites

Different SharePoint site templates include different types of lists. The lists you see in your SharePoint site may be default lists included in the template or additional lists added by the site owner.

What Makes a SharePoint List

A SharePoint list consists of columns to store and display the data required for the list, list properties such as the name of the list, the views created for the list, and behaviors configured for the list contents, such as grouping and totalling.

SharePoint Columns

SharePoint columns contain the data stored in SharePoint lists, and are similar to fields in a database. For example, columns included in a contact list might be first name, last name, phone number, and address. Columns provide flexibility for site owners and users by allowing them to include only the columns they want in a list they create, or to hide or reorganize columns to create new views of list data.

Types of Lists

The following lists are available in SharePoint 2013.

List Type	Description
Announcements	Displays short announcements. Typically used on home pages for organizations, teams, and projects. Expiration dates can be set for announcements so that the list remains current.
Calendar	Provides familiar day, week, month calendar views and stores calendar items such as meetings, events, vacations, and holidays. Often used for team and project calendars.

List Type	Description
Contacts	Stores and organizes typical contact information. Your SharePoint site might have multiple contact lists for internal contacts, partner contacts, vendor contacts, and customer contacts.
Discussion Board	Creates a threaded discussion board where people can post and reply to questions. Often used in corporate, departmental, team, and project sites to facilitate discussion on matters of interest.
Links	Stores URLs (hyperlinks). These links may be on internal intranet sites, or external sites on the Internet and are any links that people feel are useful. Links may be used to store a list of all the key internal websites for an organization, or websites of key partners when used in a project site.
Issue Tracking	Tracks support tickets (also known as trouble tickets or support requests) for an organization. This list allows you to follow the progress of the issue until the issue is resolved and closed. This list is often used on help desk sites to track support issues.
Survey	Used to take polls, this list records and tracks responses to a specific list of questions. Survey lists usually collect feedback in areas of long term interest to the organization, such as employee feedback on corporate policies, or customer feedback on help desk services.
Tasks	Stores task items. This list is often use to store tasks, action items, and due dates for departments, teams or projects. The task list can be synchronized with Microsoft® Outlook® to allow users to add and work with tasks through either interface.
Custom	A list composed of columns, a default list view, and behaviors created by the site owner. Custom lists may be created for any number of reasons where the default lists available in SharePoint don't meet user needs.
External	A list based on a data source outside of SharePoint. May be used any time the data exists outside of SharePoint to allow collaboration with that data from SharePoint.
Import Spreadsheet	Lets you create a list by importing a spreadsheet. This may be used to avoid duplicating or re-entering data.

Note: To learn more about SharePoint Issue Tracking list, refer to the LearnTO **Manage Quality Assurance Using Issue Tracking** presentation from the **LearnTO** tile on the LogicalCHOICE Course screen.

Note: To learn more about SharePoint Issue Survey list, refer to the LearnTO **Use Survey Lists to Improve Business Processes** presentation from the **LearnTO** tile on the LogicalCHOICE Course screen.

SharePoint Lists Available in Your Organization

The lists available for your SharePoint site will depend on the version of SharePoint deployed in your organization.

Access the Checklist tile on your CHOICE Course screen for reference information and job aids on How to Add List Items.

ACTIVITY 3-1
Adding an Item to a List

Before You Begin
You should be logged into the classroom SharePoint site, and your browser should have the Developer Team Site page open.

Scenario
Because this is your first day at your new company and working on your new project, your supervisor has asked you to take care of some administrative tasks. She's asked you to add your contact information to the contacts list for your project, and to schedule a New Employee Orientation meeting that she will conduct for you and other new employees hired for the project. She's also asked you to share a quality control document that you brought with you from your previous job with members of the team. Finally, she's asked you to post a link to a website you mentioned that could be useful as a reference for the project. You will add items to the lists on the Project Orange site to accomplish these tasks.

---

1. Access the Project Orange Team Site.
    a) In the **Quick Launch** area, under **Subsites**, select **Project Orange**.

2. Add your contact information to the **Orange Contacts** list.
    a) On the **Project Orange** page, select **Orange Contacts**.

    > **Note:** You may need to scroll the window in order to see **Orange Contacts** on the right side of the page.

    b) On the **Orange Contacts** page, select **new item** to display the new contact list form.
    c) In the **Last Name** box, type *<Your User Name>*
    d) In the **Email Address** box, type *<Your User Name>@develetech.com*
    e) In the **Company Name** box, type **Develetech**
    f) In the **Business Phone** box, type a phone number.
    g) Select **Save**.

    > **Note:** You can use the **Save** button at the bottom of the page or the one on the **EDIT** ribbon tab.

    h) Observe your contact information in the list.

Last Name	First Name	Company	Business Phone	Home Phone	Email Address
Francis	Henry	Develetech	(555) 555-1254	(555) 555-1234	henryf@develetech.com
Ortega	Mia	Develetech	(555) 555-1252	(555) 555-2323	miaor@develetech.com
Sanderson	Cory	Develetech	(555) 555-1250	(555) 555-5678	corys@develetech.com
Student2		Develetech	(555) 555-1928		student2@develetech.com

    i) In the **Quick Launch** area, select **Project Orange Home**.

3. Add a new task to the Orange Tasks list.
    a) On the **Project Orange** page, select **Orange Tasks**.

b) On the **Orange Tasks** page, select **new task**.

Orange Tasks ⓘ

Today

March 2013   April 2013

Add tasks with dates to the tim

(+) new task or edit this list

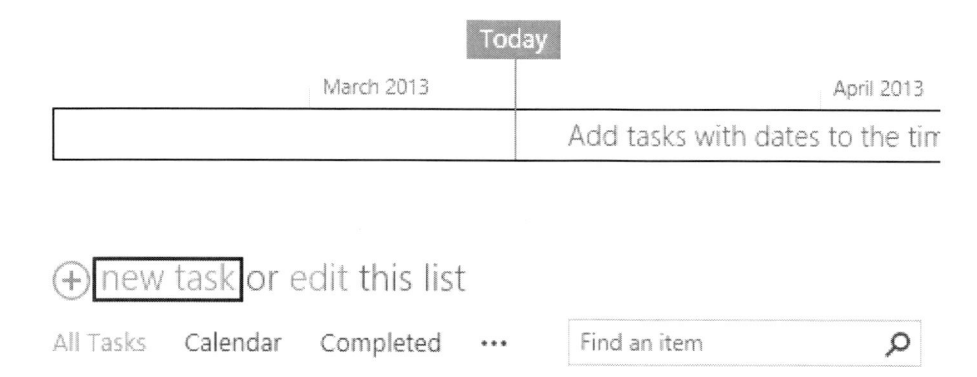

All Tasks   Calendar   Completed   ···   Find an item

c) In the **Task Name** box, type *<Your User Name> New Employee Orientation*
d) Next to **Start Date** select the **Calendar**

button.

e) On the calendar that appears, select the date for the following **Monday** from today's date.

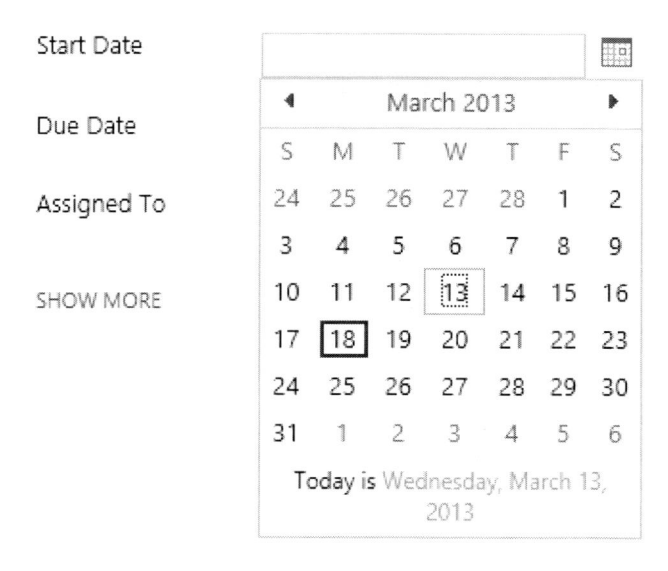

Start Date							
Due Date	◀		March 2013			▶	
	S	M	T	W	T	F	S
Assigned To	24	25	26	27	28	1	2
	3	4	5	6	7	8	9
SHOW MORE	10	11	12	13	14	15	16
	17	18	19	20	21	22	23
	24	25	26	27	28	29	30
	31	1	2	3	4	5	6

Today is Wednesday, March 13, 2013

f) Next to **Due Date**, select the **Calendar** button.
g) On the calendar that appears, select the date for the following **Monday** from today's date.
h) In the **Assigned To** box, type *ShellyS; <Your User Name>*
i) Select **Save**.
j) In the **Quick Launch** area, select **Project Orange Home**.

4. Add an announcement to **Orange Announcements**.
    a) On the **Project Orange** page, select **Orange Announcements**.

> **Note:** You may need to scroll the window in order to see **Orange Announcements**.

b) On the **Orange Announcements** page, on the ribbon, select the **ITEMS** tab.
c) Observe the options available on the **ITEMS** tab.

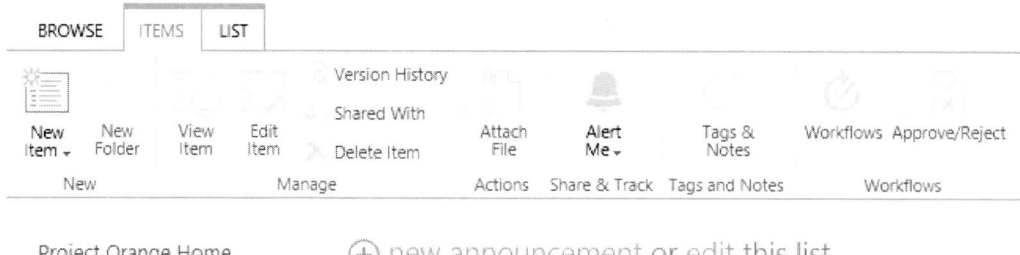

d) On the **ITEMS** tab, select **New Item**.
e) In the **Title** box type, *Quality Control document from <Your User Name>*
f) In the **Body** box type, *Shelly wanted me to share a quality control procedure document I brought with me from my previous job. It's on my desk.*
g) Select **Save**.
h) Observe your new announcement in the announcements list.
i) In the **Quick Launch** area, select **Project Orange Home**.

5. Add a link to Orange Links.
   a) On the **Project Orange** page, select **Orange Links**.

   > **Note:** You may need to scroll the window in order to see **Orange Links**.

   b) On the **Orange Links** page, select **new link**.
   c) In the **URL** box type *http://<Your User Name>projecttesting.com*

   d) In the **Type the description** box, type *Good site from <Your User Name>*
   e) Select **Save**.
   f) Observe your link in the **Orange Links** list.
   g) In the **Navigation** pane, select **Project Orange Home**.
   h) Observe your link in the **Orange Links** list on the home page (scroll to the right if necessary).

TOPIC B

Modify List Items

Although some of the data stored in SharePoint lists doesn't change very often, much of the data stored, such as contact information or calendar events, may need to be updated frequently. In this topic you will modify items in SharePoint lists.

List and List Item Modification Options

SharePoint lists and list items can be modified in much the same way you can modify any database or spreadsheet. Users who are members of the site, or who have the contributor permission level or greater, can add and delete items from lists or edit items. When modifying list items and events, you will use the same forms used to add items. In the item properties you can update information text boxes, date fields, categories, and any information associated with the item or event, and then save those changes.

> **Access the Checklist tile on your CHOICE Course screen for reference information and job aids on How to Modify List Items.**

ACTIVITY 3-2
Modifying List Items

Before You Begin

You should be logged into the classroom SharePoint site, and your browser should have the Project Orange home page open.

Scenario

As you continue your first day, there have been some new requests and changes. First, the site owner has asked you to remove the link you recently added siting some firewall concerns. Your supervisor asked you to setup an email alert for changes in the New Employee Orientation meeting because it is becoming quite large. She has asked you to move the meeting to start one day later. She also asked you to make sure that the meeting is added to the Project Orange Timeline on the home page. Then you saw some discussion items that you wished to reply to, and you should verify that your email alert is working.

1. Delete the link you created in Orange Links.
    a) On the **Project Orange** home page, select **Orange Links** to open the **Orange Links** list.
    b) In the **Orange Links** list, next to **Good Site from <Your User Name>**, select the **Open Menu** button to open the menu.

    > **Note:** You may need to scroll to the right to see the **Open Menu** button.

c) Observe the actions available on the menu.

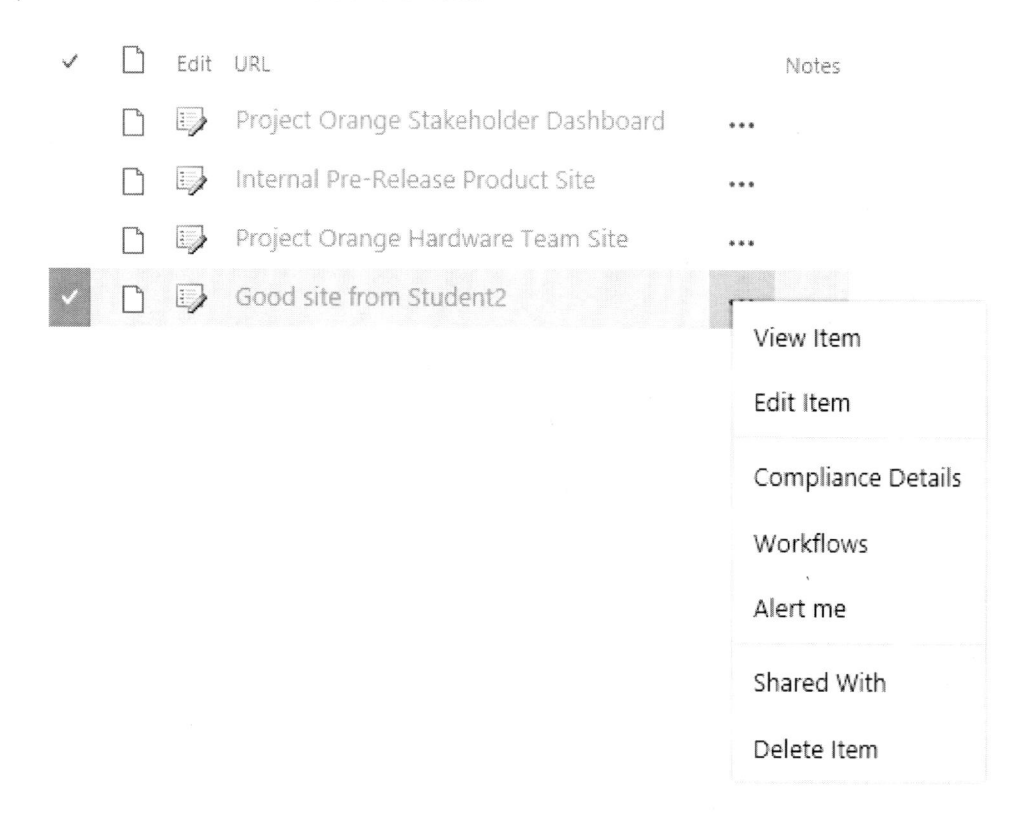

✓		Edit	URL		Notes
			Project Orange Stakeholder Dashboard	...	
			Internal Pre-Release Product Site	...	
			Project Orange Hardware Team Site	...	
✓			Good site from Student2		

- View Item
- Edit Item
- Compliance Details
- Workflows
- Alert me
- Shared With
- Delete Item

d) Select **Delete Item**.
e) In the **Message from webpage** dialog box that appears asking if you are sure, select **OK**.

> **Note:** This will move the item to the site recycle bin. The site recycle bin will be covered in more detail in a later lesson.

f) Observe the results in the **Orange Links** list.

Orange Links ⓘ

(+) new link or edit this list

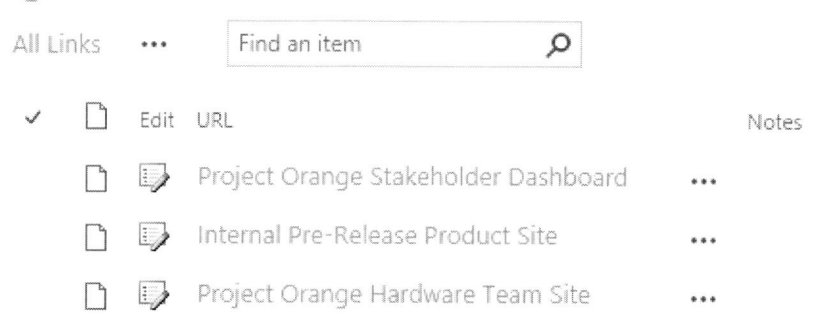

All Links ··· [Find an item   🔍]

✓		Edit	URL		Notes
			Project Orange Stakeholder Dashboard	...	
			Internal Pre-Release Product Site	...	
			Project Orange Hardware Team Site	...	

2. Set an alert for the New Employee Orientation meeting.
   a) In the **Quick Launch** area, select **Project Orange Home**.
   b) In the **Orange Tasks** list, select the **<Your User Name> New Employee Orientation** document name.

In the preceding step, you need to select the document name, not check the check box to see the **BROWSE** and **VIEW** tabs.

c) On the ribbon **VIEW** tab, in the **Actions** group, select **Alert Me**.
d) In the **New Alert** page, verify the **Alert Title**.

> **Note:** The **Alert Title** should be **Orange Tasks: <Your User Name> New Employee Orientation**.

e) In the **Delivery Method** section, verify that **Send me alerts by** is set to **E-Mail**.

> **Note:** Observe that you can also send notifications by text message.

f) In the **Send Alerts for These Changes** section, under **Send me an alert when**, verify that **Anything changes** is selected.

> **Note:** You can also generate alerts when someone else changes an item, someone else changes and item created by you, someone else changes an item last modified by you, and someone changes an item that appears on the following view.

g) In the **When to send alerts** section, verify that **Send notification immediately** is selected.
h) Select **OK** to save the alert.

3. Edit your New Employee Orientation task.
    a) In the **Orange Tasks** list, next to **<Your User Name> New Employee Orientation**, select the **Open Menu** button.
    b) In the item window, select **Add to Timeline**.

c) Observe the timeline view in the page.

Orange Tasks

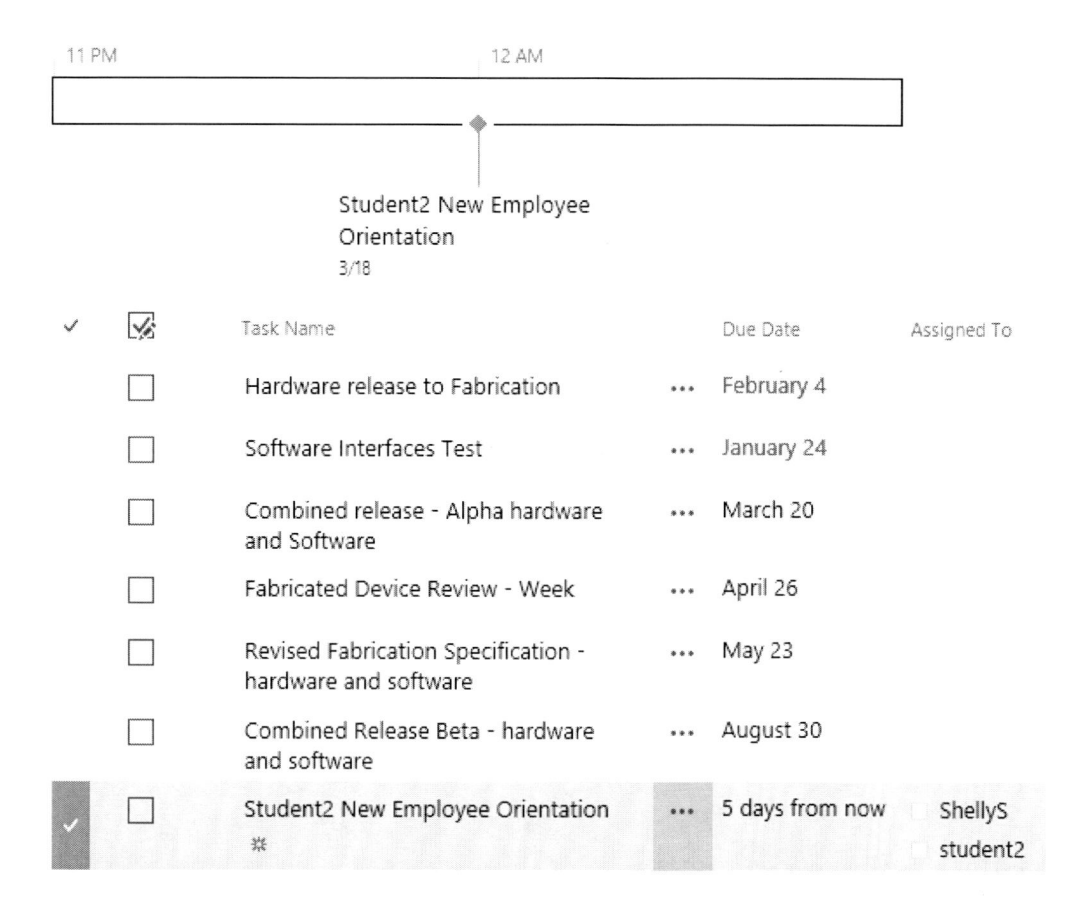

		Task Name	Due Date	Assigned To
		Hardware release to Fabrication	February 4	
		Software Interfaces Test	January 24	
		Combined release - Alpha hardware and Software	March 20	
		Fabricated Device Review - Week	April 26	
		Revised Fabrication Specification - hardware and software	May 23	
		Combined Release Beta - hardware and software	August 30	
✓		Student2 New Employee Orientation	5 days from now	ShellyS student2

Timeline shows: Student2 New Employee Orientation 3/18

d) In the **Orange Tasks** list, next to **<Your User Name> New Employee Orientation**, select the **Open Menu** button.
e) In the item window, select the **Open Menu** button, and then select **Edit Item**.
f) Next to **Start Date,** select the **Calendar** button.
g) In the **Calendar,** select a date that is one day later.

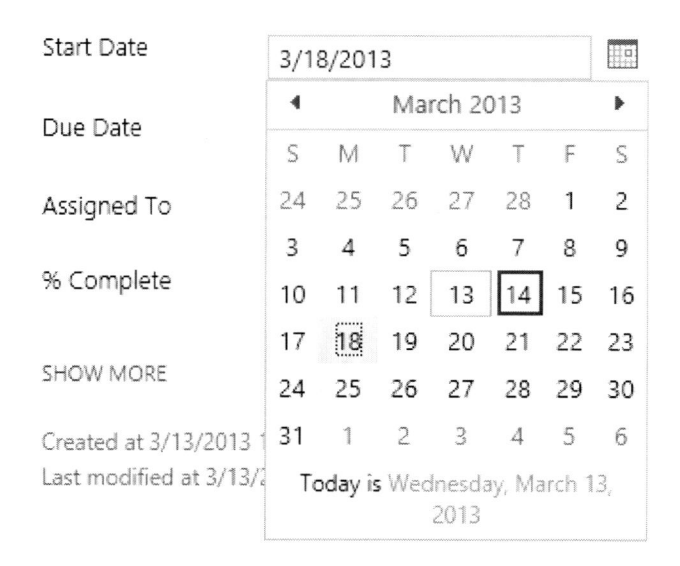

Start Date: 3/18/2013

March 2013 calendar showing today is Wednesday, March 13, 2013; 18 is highlighted, 14 is boxed.

Fields shown: Start Date, Due Date, Assigned To, % Complete, SHOW MORE

Created at 3/13/2013
Last modified at 3/13/2

h) Next to **Due Date**, select the **Calendar** button.
i) In the **Calendar**, select a date that is one day later.
j) Select **Save.**
k) Observe the timeline has been updated.

Orange Tasks

11 PM   12 AM

Student2 New Employee
Orientation
3/14

l) In the Quick Launch area, select **Project Orange Home.**

4. Reply to a discussion.
    a) In the **Orange Discussion** list, select the **SDK Samples for API** link.

    > **Note:** You may need to scroll the window in order to see **Orange Discussion**.

    b) On the **SDK Samples for API** page, in the **Add a reply** box, type *<Your User Name> A single SDK sample for each major API category.*
    c) Select **Reply.**
    d) Observe your reply in the list.

    Administrator
    Should we have a single SDK sample for each major API catetory or multiple smaller samples?
    Monday at 4:28 PM   Reply   Alert me

    All replies
    Oldest   Newest

    student2
    Student2 A single SDK sample for each major API category.
    A few seconds ago   Reply   Edit   ...

    e) In the **Quick Launch** area, select **Project Orange Home.**
    f) Observe the **Orange Discussion** list.

    > **Note:** You can not see your reply on the home page. To see replies you have to open the list and the discussion itself.

5. Open Outlook to view alerts from SharePoint.
    a) Open **Outlook.**
    b) Your mailbox appears. If you receive a certificate error, select **Yes.**

> **Note:** You should have received two messages from Project Orange.

c) In Outlook, select the oldest message from **Project Orange** and view it in the reading pane.

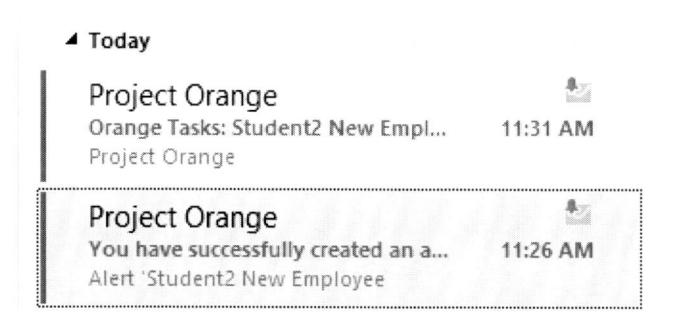

▲ Today

    Project Orange
    Orange Tasks: Student2 New Empl...   11:31 AM
    Project Orange

    Project Orange
    You have successfully created an a...   11:26 AM
    Alert 'Student2 New Employee

> **Note:** The oldest message should be informing you that you have created an alert for <Your User Name> New Employee Orientation.

d) In Outlook, select the latest message from **Project Orange.**

▲ Today

    Project Orange
    Orange Tasks: Student2 New Empl...   11:31 AM
    Project Orange

    Project Orange
    You have successfully created an al... 11:26 AM
    Alert 'Student2 New Employee

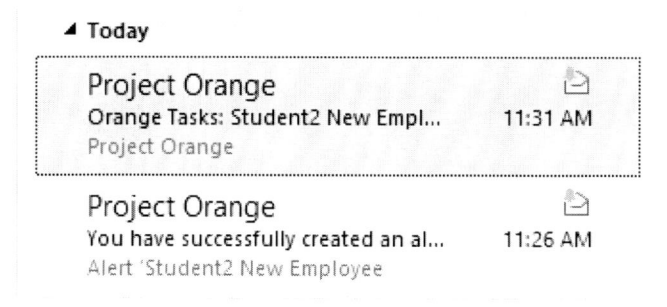

e) In the Outlook preview pane, scroll down to see the entire contents of the message.

> **Note:** This message should be informing you that <Your User Name> New Employee Orientation has been changed.

f) Minimize Outlook and switch to your browser.
g) In the **Quick Launch** area, select **Project Orange Home**.

TOPIC C

Configure List Views

If you work with SharePoint lists frequently, it is often helpful to be able to customize the list view so that you can see the data that you're interested in, presented in the way that is most helpful to you. In this topic you will create and modify list views in SharePoint.

List Views

A *list view* defines how the items in the list are displayed. The view may define specific columns that are displayed and their order, or may provide other visualizations such as a calendar for viewing schedules, or Gantt Chart for viewing project tasks. Every list has at least one view, this is often the **All Items** view, and may have additional views that you can choose from. Every list has a default view. You can select from available views to customize the way list data is displayed, or customize views to add, remove, or reorganize columns that are displayed. You can also create new views for yourself or to share with your team. Adding and changing views does not affect the information stored in the list, only how it is displayed.

Library Views

Libraries also have views. You can create and customize library views the same as you can for lists. By default, document libraries start with the **All Documents** view.

List View Audience

There are two categories of list views available in each SharePoint Site.

View Category	Description
Public	Is available for anyone who has access to the list.
Personal	Is only available for the team member who created the view.

Mobile Views

SharePoint 2013 supports access by mobile devices, such as smart phones and tablet computers. Any public view can be enabled for mobile access. If it is enabled, and the list is viewed on a mobile device, SharePoint will format the list view for the smaller screens of mobile devices.

List View Types

When you create a new view in SharePoint 2013, you can use an existing view, or one of the view types as a starting point. The following view types are available in SharePoint 2013.

View Type	Description
Standard	Displays the list on a web page, the items in the list are displayed similarly to items in a table with no borders showing. This view is common for list where data doesn't change often such as contact lists.
Datasheet	Displays data in a spreadsheet, allowing users to navigate with arrow keys, select rows or columns, and is generally used for providing faster editing and customization of list data.

View Type	Description
Calendar	Displays data in a calendar view and provides day, week, month, and other options typical to calendars. You must have at least one date field in your list to use this view.
Gantt	A *Gantt Chart* displays data in a graphical, tasks over time format used in many project management charts. This view is the default for the Tasks list, and is often used with other task lists.
Access	Creates an Access® database. The tables linked to SharePoint lists allow users to create forms and reports in Access based on the SharePoint list.
Custom View in SharePoint Designer	Allows you to create custom views using SharePoint Designer.

Default List Views

The following table contains list types and their associated views in SharePoint 2013.

List Type	Views
Announcements	All Items
Calendar	Calendar, All Events, and Current Events
Contacts	All Contacts
Discussion Board	Subject, Featured Discussions, and Management
Links	All Links
Issue Tracking	All Issues, Active Issues, and My Issues
Survey	Survey
Tasks	All Tasks, Calendar, Completed, Gantt Chart, Late Tasks, My Tasks, and Upcoming
External	All Items

List View Settings

When you create or modify a view, you have to select the settings for that view, including the name of the view, the columns to include, their order, how items should be sorted and so forth. The following table describes the list view settings available in SharePoint.

Setting	Description
Name	Name of the list. There is also an option to make the view the default view for the list.
Audience	Enables you to select whether this is a personal or public view.
Columns	Determines what columns will be displayed in the view, and in what order in relation to each other.
Sort	Allows you to select up to two columns to sort by and lets you specify an ascending or descending sort.
Filter	Lets you refine the items displayed in the view based on criteria that you define.

Setting	Description
Tabular View	Determines whether check boxes will be displayed for each row in the list. Check boxes allow you to select multiple items to perform bulk operations.
Group By	Enables you to select up to two columns to group by for grouping and subgrouping options. Grouping is useful to display data in ways that is more meaningful and easy to navigate, such as grouping contacts by City or State.
Totals	Allows you to display one or more totals for columns in the list.
Style	Lets you choose a style for the list to control how data is displayed.
Folders	Allows you to display items either in their folders (if folders are present) or hide folders and display all items in a flat list.
Item Limit	Enables you to limit the number of items displayed at once, or in total for the list. This is used to display list items in batches when there are many items.
Mobile	Allows you to make public views available for mobile devices and to set a public view as the default mobile view. It also lets you set a separate item limit entry for mobile devices.

List Display Styles

By default, SharePoint displays list data in rows, much like a table without the borders showing. List display styles allow you to change the default display to customize a list or a view. The following table lists the list display styles available.

Display Style	Description
Basic	Displays items in a table without visible rows with most buttons removed.
Boxed	Displays data as a series of cards like address cards with column headings visible on the left of each card.
Boxed, No Labels	Same as the **Boxed** display style but without the column headings visible.
Newsletter	A streamlined view separated by lines on the page, with buttons such as **New** and **Open Menu** removed from the content area.
Newsletter, No Lines	Same as **Newsletter** but without the lines separating each item in the list.
Shaded	Displays a table with alternate rows shaded.
Preview Pane	Displays the item name on the left and the item details on the right. Move the mouse pointer over the item names to see their details.
Default	The default style for the type of list.

> **Note:** At the time of publication, there appears to be a bug in SharePoint 2013 with regard to the **Newsletter, No Lines** style. This style is currently displaying the **Shaded** style when selected.

Note: To learn more about SharePoint Display Styles, refer to the LearnTO **Review Display Styles** presentation from the **LearnTO** tile on the LogicalCHOICE Course screen.

Access the Checklist tile on your CHOICE Course screen for reference information and job aids on How to Change and Save List Views.

ACTIVITY 3-3
Modifying and Saving List Views

Before You Begin
You should be logged into the classroom SharePoint site, and your browser should have the Project Orange Home page open.

Scenario
As you continue to use your SharePoint team site, you've decided that you want to change some of the views on some of the lists, to help you work the way you like, and see the information presented differently. In addition, your supervisor has asked you to extend the New Employee Orientation meeting. You will create and modify some views for lists in the Project Orange site and observe the results.

1. Change your default view for Orange Contacts to **Datasheet View**.
    a) On the **Project Orange** home page, select **Orange Contacts**.
    b) On the ribbon, select the **LIST** tab, then in the **Manage Views** group, select **Create View**.

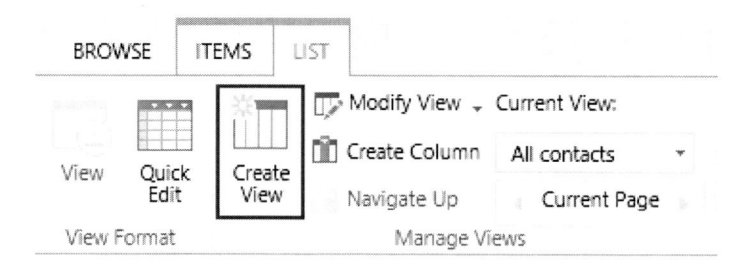

    c) On the **View Type** page, observe the types of views available.
    d) Select **Datasheet View**.
    e) On the **Create View** page, in the **View Name** box, type *<Your User Name> Datasheet*
    f) In the **Audience** section, select **Create a Personal View**.

    > **Note:** In this activity, you will be creating personal views. You will see that there is an option to make a view the default view. Because only public views can be made default views, you will not be able to make the views that you create default views.

    g) Select **OK**.
    h) Observe the new view in the **Orange Contacts** list.

2. Navigate in **Datasheet View** using arrow keys.

a) Select the cell with the **Last Name** of **Francis**.

Orange Contacts

Stop editing this list

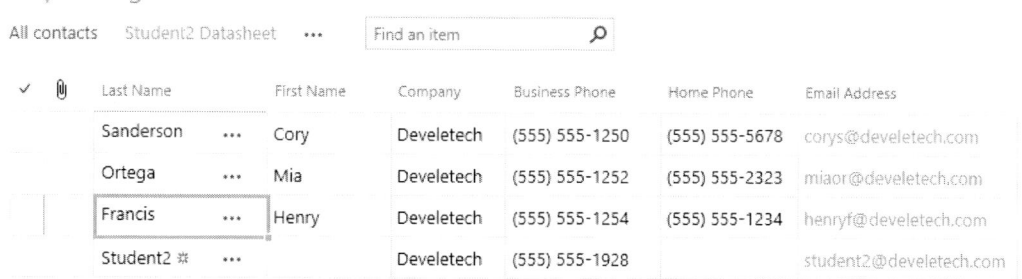

All contacts   Student2 Datasheet   ···   Find an item

		Last Name	First Name	Company	Business Phone	Home Phone	Email Address
✓	📎						
		Sanderson ···	Cory	Develetech	(555) 555-1250	(555) 555-5678	corys@develetech.com
		Ortega ···	Mia	Develetech	(555) 555-1252	(555) 555-2323	miaor@develetech.com
		Francis ···	Henry	Develetech	(555) 555-1254	(555) 555-1234	henryf@develetech.com
		Student2 ✴ ···		Develetech	(555) 555-1928		student2@develetech.com

> **Note:** Click inside the cell, but do not click the text in the cell. If you click the text in the cell you will be editing the contact. In this activity you just want to move around the **Datasheet View** using the arrow keys.

b) Press the arrow keys to move the cell selector to different cells.
c) Select the **Last Name** column header to re-sort the datasheet by last name.

> **Note:** Select the text of the name to sort the list. If you select outside the text you will get a drop-down menu with options to select or sort.

3. Observe the differences in list views.
    a) In the **Orange Contacts** list menu bar, select **All contacts** and observe the change in list view.

Orange Contacts

Stop editing this list

[All contacts]   Student2 Datasheet   ···   Find an item   SAVE THIS VIEW

b) In the **Orange Contacts** list menu bar, select **<YourUserName> Datasheet** and observe the change in list view.
c) In the **Quick Launch** area, select **Project Orange Home**.

> **Note:** If there are more than three views you will have to select the **Open Menu** button to show all available views.

d) Observe the **Orange Contacts** List.

> **Note:** The view of **Orange Contacts** from the homepage is still the **All Contacts** view because the **Project Orange** page view has not been changed.

4. Add views to the **Orange Tasks** list.
    a) On the **Project Orange** page, select **Orange Tasks**.
    b) On the ribbon, select the **LIST** tab, then in the **Manage Views** group, select **Create View**.
    c) On the **View Type** page, select **Gantt View**.
    d) On the **Create View** page, in the **View Name** box, type *<Your User Name> Gantt*
    e) In the **Audience** section, select **Create a Personal View**.
    f) In the **Gantt Columns** section, in the **Title** drop-down menu, select **Task Name**.

> Note: You may need to scroll down in order to see the **Gantt Columns** section.

g) In the **Start Date** drop-down list, select **Start Date**.
h) In the **Due Date** drop-down list, select **Due Date**.
i) Select **OK**.

> Note: You will need to scroll to the top or the bottom of the page in order to see the **OK** button.

j) Observe the new view in the **Orange Tasks** list.

Orange Tasks

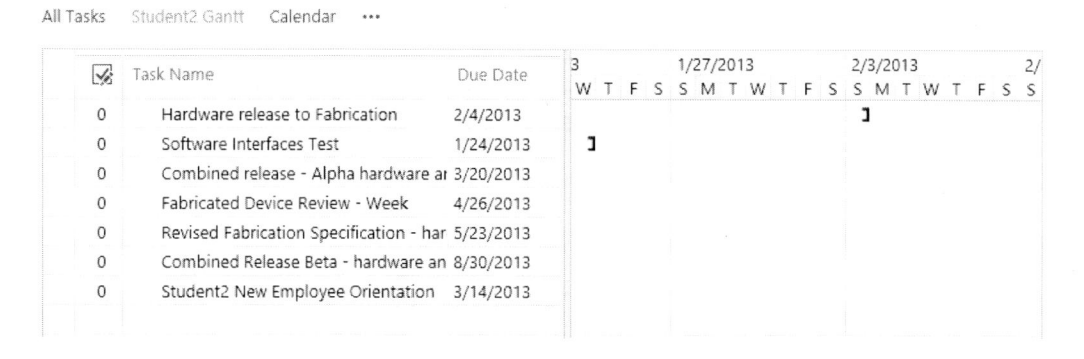

Task Name	Due Date
Hardware release to Fabrication	2/4/2013
Software Interfaces Test	1/24/2013
Combined release - Alpha hardware ar	3/20/2013
Fabricated Device Review - Week	4/26/2013
Revised Fabrication Specification - har	5/23/2013
Combined Release Beta - hardware an	8/30/2013
Student2 New Employee Orientation	3/14/2013

5. Update tasks and view changes.
    a) Next to **<Your User Name> New Employee Orientation**, select the **Due Date** cell.

   > Note: You may need to scroll the task details area in order to see the **Due Date** column.

    b) A **Calendar** button appears next to the **Due Date** cell. Select the **Calendar** button.

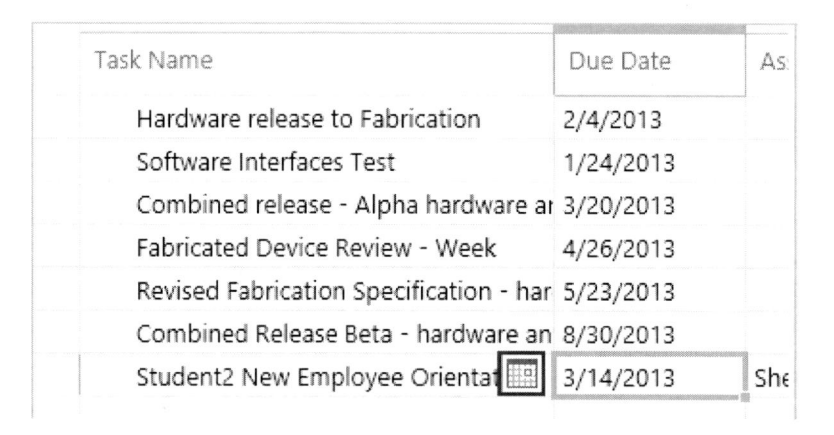

Task Name	Due Date
Hardware release to Fabrication	2/4/2013
Software Interfaces Test	1/24/2013
Combined release - Alpha hardware ar	3/20/2013
Fabricated Device Review - Week	4/26/2013
Revised Fabrication Specification - har	5/23/2013
Combined Release Beta - hardware an	8/30/2013
Student2 New Employee Orienta	3/14/2013

    c) In the calendar, select the Thursday following the current end date.
    d) Select any other task name from the task list to update the task.
    e) Observe the updated Gantt Chart.
    f) On the ribbon, select the **LIST** tab, then in the **Gantt View** group, select **Zoom In** twice.
    g) Observe the Gantt chart.
    h) In the **LIST** tab, in the **Gantt View** group, select **Zoom Out** twice.

6. Observe views available.

a) In the **LIST** tab, in the **Manage Views** group, select the **Current View** drop-down list.

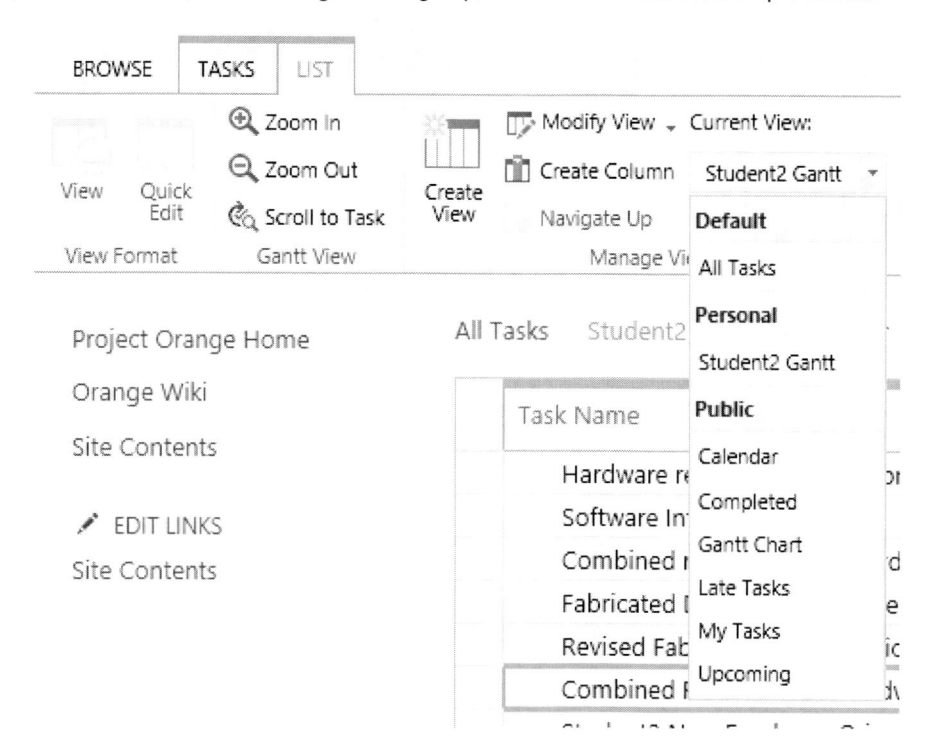

b) In the **Change View** drop-down list, under **Public**, select **Calendar**.
c) In the Calendar, select **<Your User Name> New Employee Orientation** to open the task.

d) Observe the task, and select **Close**.
e) In the Calendar, select the day on which the **<Your User Name> New Employee Orientation** starts.

> **Note:** To open the day view from the month view of the calendar, you must select either the date number or in the top portion of the calendar cell.

f) Observe the calendar day view.
g) On the ribbon, select the **CALENDAR** tab, then in the **Scope** group, select **Week**.
h) Observe the week view.
i) On the ribbon, select the **LIST** tab, then in the **Manage Views** group, select the **Current View** drop-down list, and select **<Your User Name> Gantt**.
j) Observe the change in view.

7. Review alerts in Outlook.
    a) Switch to **Outlook**.

b) Select the most recent message from Project Orange.

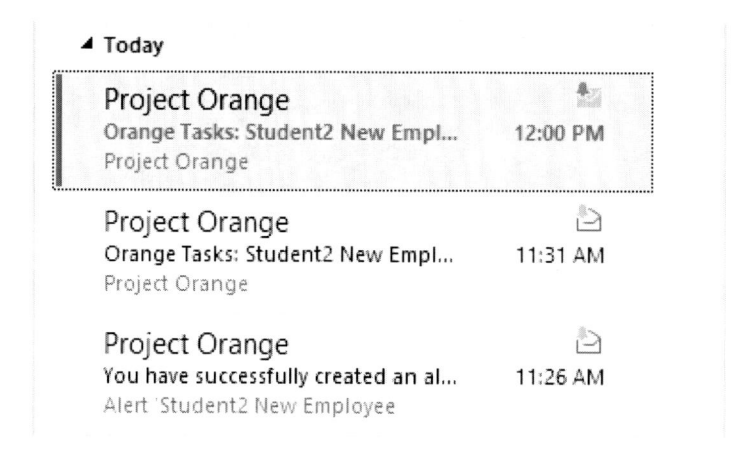

```
▲ Today

┌─────────────────────────────────────────────────┐
│ Project Orange                                  │
│ Orange Tasks: Student2 New Empl...    12:00 PM  │
│ Project Orange                                  │
└─────────────────────────────────────────────────┘

  Project Orange
  Orange Tasks: Student2 New Empl...    11:31 AM
  Project Orange

  Project Orange
  You have successfully created an al... 11:26 AM
  Alert 'Student2 New Employee
```

> **Note:** You should receive an alert from Project Orange that the <Your User Name> New Employee Orientation has been changed.

c) Switch to your web browser.
d) In **SharePoint** in the **Quick Launch** area, select **Project Orange Home.**

TOPIC D

Filter and Group with List Views

At times it is helpful to filter list results or group list data by specific columns in order to get a list view that is more helpful or easier to use. In this topic you will filter and group list views.

List Filtering Options

SharePoint gives you the option to filter list results as part of a list view to show only items that meet a specified criteria. Your filter can specify a single criteria, or two criteria to create an "and/or" filter. For example, if a salesperson is searching for contacts in their sales region, they might create a view that filters a contact list first by their sales region, and then by specific states within that region.

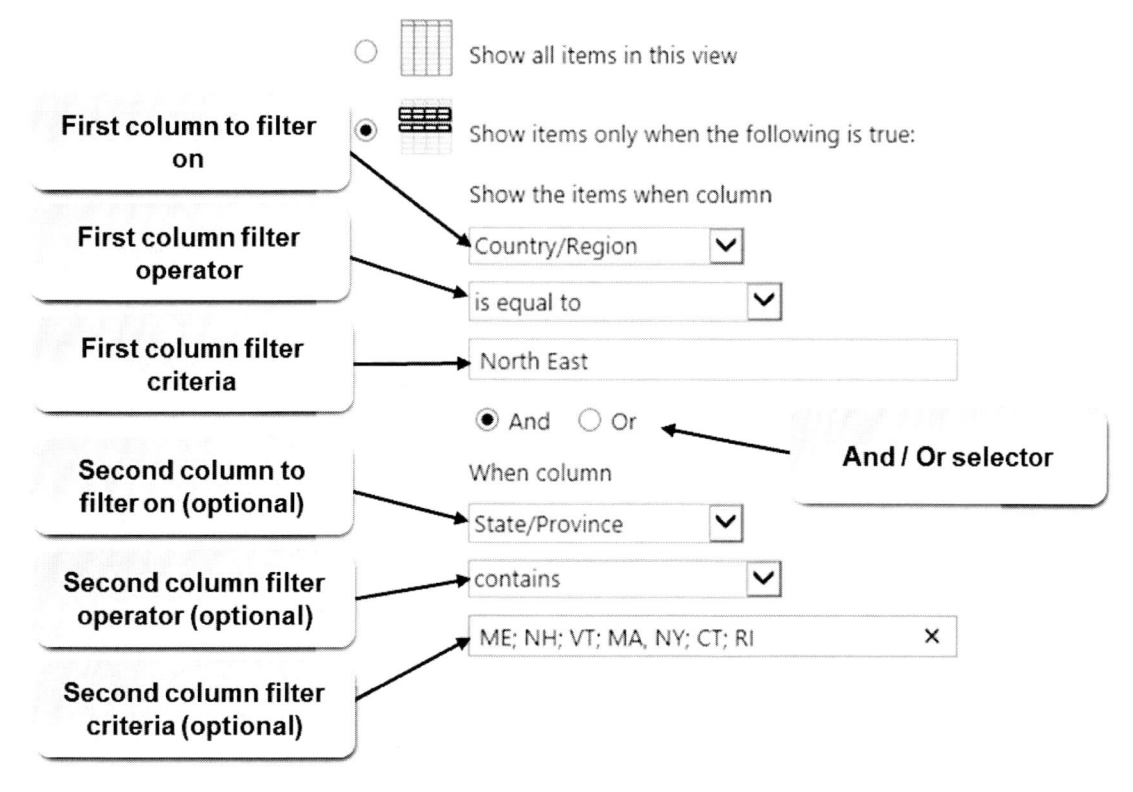

Figure 3-1: The list filtering options.

Filter Operators Available in SharePoint Filters

The following operators are available in SharePoint filters:

- Is equal to
- Is not equal to
- Is greater than
- Is less than
- Is greater than or equal to
- Is less than or equal to
- Begins with
- Contains

List Grouping Options

SharePoint gives you the option to group list results as part of a list view to organize items in a more meaningful way, or allow for quicker navigation through large lists. You can group by a single column, or by a first column, and then by a second column to create subgroups beneath the first grouping. For example, in a contact list, you might group first by State or Province, and then by City.

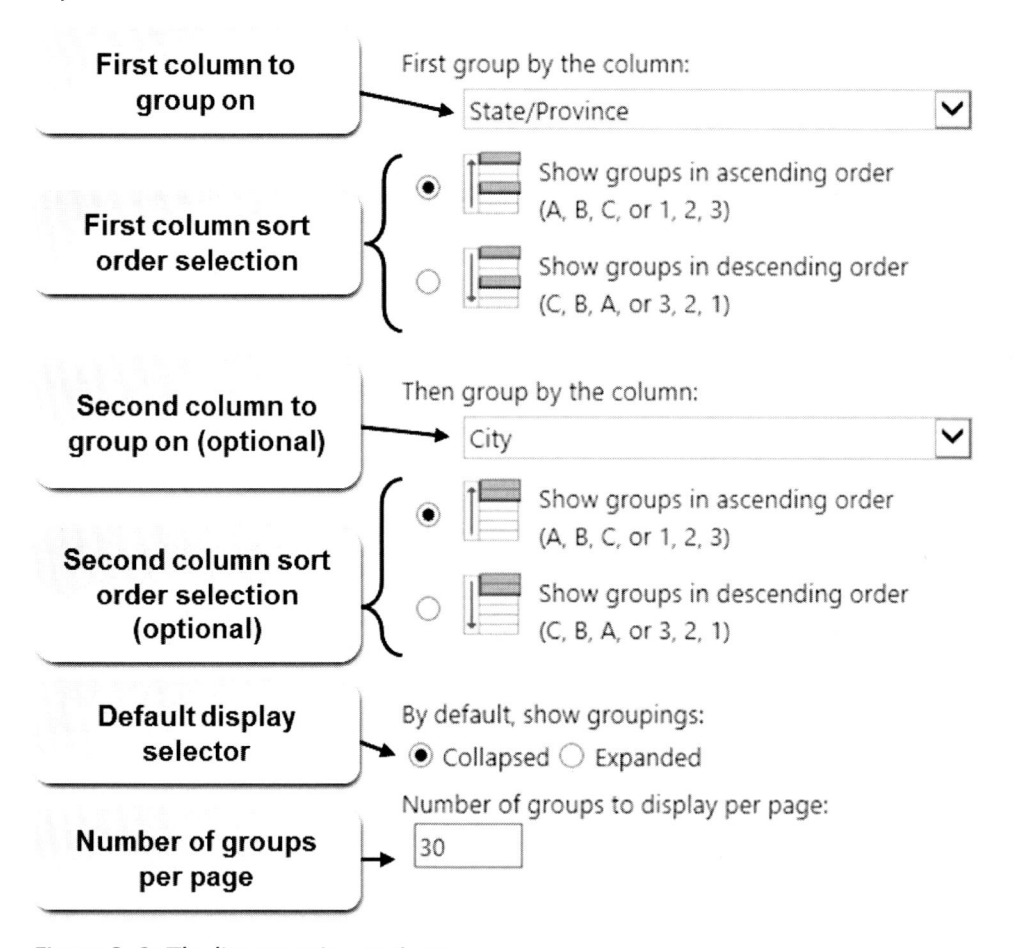

First column to group on	First group by the column: State/Province
First column sort order selection	● Show groups in ascending order (A, B, C, or 1, 2, 3) ○ Show groups in descending order (C, B, A, or 3, 2, 1)
Second column to group on (optional)	Then group by the column: City
Second column sort order selection (optional)	● Show groups in ascending order (A, B, C, or 1, 2, 3) ○ Show groups in descending order (C, B, A, or 3, 2, 1)
Default display selector	By default, show groupings: ● Collapsed ○ Expanded
Number of groups per page	Number of groups to display per page: 30

Figure 3-2: The list grouping options.

> Access the Checklist tile on your **CHOICE** Course screen for reference information and job aids on **How to Organize Columns and Filter and Group List Views.**

ACTIVITY 3-4
Working with Columns, Filtering, and Grouping

Before You Begin
You should be logged into the classroom SharePoint site, and your browser should have the Project Orange home page open.

Scenario
Now that you've changed some of the views in the lists you use frequently, you would like to make additional modifications to the information that is displayed and how it is displayed. For contacts, you want to see additional columns that have information you want, and you would like to filter and group both the contacts and task lists to see the information that is most important to you. In this activity, you will work with columns, filtering, and grouping to modify your list views.

1. Add and remove columns to your contacts view.
    a) On the **Project Orange** home page, select **Orange Contacts**.
    b) On the **Orange Contacts** page, on the ribbon, select the **LIST** tab, then in the **Manage Views** group, select **Modify View**.
    c) In the **Columns** section, uncheck the **Attachments** check box.
    d) Uncheck the **Home Phone** box.
    e) Check the following check boxes: **City, Country/Region, Fax Number, State/Province**.

2. Sort the view.
    a) In Sort section, in the **First sort by the column** drop-down menu, select **Last Name (linked to item with edit menu)**.
    b) Verify that **Show items in ascending order** is selected.
    c) In the **Then sort by the column** drop-down list, select **First Name**.
    The Last Name and First name columns may already be selected, if so, continue to the next step.
    d) Verify that **Show items in ascending order** is selected.
    e) Scroll to the bottom of the page and select **OK**.
    f) Observe the modified view.

    > **Note:** Observe that the new columns are displayed in the datasheet, but that State/Province does not immediately follow City. Some reordering of the columns is in order.

3. Rearrange column position in the view.
    a) On the ribbon, select the **LIST** tab, then in the **Manage Views** group, select **Modify View**.

b) On the **Edit View** page, in the **Columns** section, observe the **Position from Left** assigned to the **City** column.

Display	Column Name	Position from Left
✓	Last Name (linked to item with edit menu)	1
✓	First Name	2
✓	Company	3
✓	Business Phone	4
✓	Email Address	5
✓	City	6
✓	Country/Region	7
✓	Fax Number	8
✓	State/Province	9
☐	Address	10

c) Next to **State/Province,** in the **Position from Left** drop-down list, select a position that immediately follows the **City** column position.

> **Note:** Observe that when you updated the State/Province position, that the Country/Region and Fax Number positions also updated.

d) Select **OK.**
e) On the **Orange Contacts** page, observe the modified view.
f) In the **Quick Launch** area, select **Project Orange Home.**

4. Create a filtered tasks view.
    a) On the **Project Orange** page, select **Orange Tasks.**
    b) On the ribbon, select the **LIST** tab, then in the **Manage Views** group, select **Modify View.**
    c) On the **Edit View** page, in the **Filter** section, select **Show items only when the following is true.**
    d) Under **Show the items when column,** in the first drop-down menu, select **Assigned To.**
    e) In the second drop-down list, verify **is equal to** is selected.
    f) Under the second drop-down list, in the text box type *<Your User Name>*

    Show the items when column
    Assigned To
    is equal to
    Student2

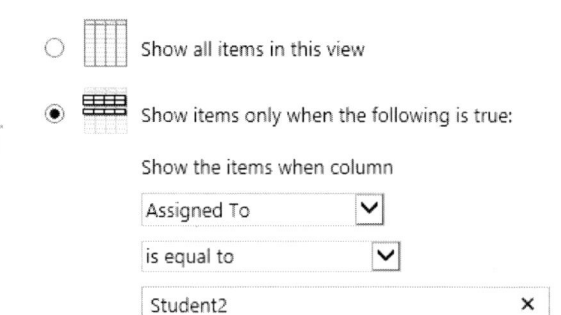

    g) Scroll to the bottom of the page and select **OK.**

h) Observe the modified view.

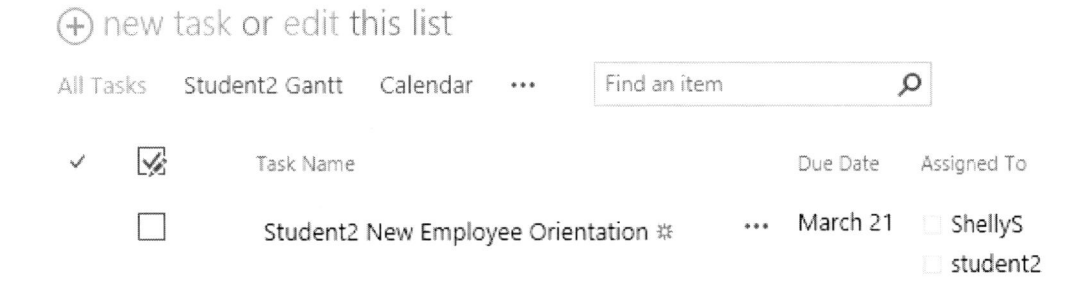

```
(+) new task or edit this list

All Tasks    Student2 Gantt    Calendar    ···    Find an item

    ✓    ☑          Task Name                              Due Date    Assigned To
         ☐          Student2 New Employee Orientation ✴  ···  March 21   ShellyS
                                                                         student2
```

i) In the **Quick Launch** area, select **Project Orange Home**.

5. Group the contacts list by city.
    a) On the **Project Orange** page, select **Orange Contacts**.
    b) On the **Orange Contacts** page, select the **<Your User Name> Datasheet** view. (Select the **LIST** tab. On the ribbon in the **Manage Views** group, select the drop-down list that currently says **All Contacts** and then choose **<Your User Name> Datasheet**.)
    c) On the ribbon, select the **LIST** tab, then in the **Manage Views** group, select **Modify View**.
    d) On the **Edit View** page, scroll down to the bottom of the page.

    > **Note:** Note that there is no **Group By** option in this view because datasheet views do not support grouping.

    e) Select **Cancel**.

6. Create a new view to group by.
    a) On the ribbon, select the **LIST** tab, then in the **Manage Views** group, select **Create View**.
    b) On the **Settings View Type** page, under **Start from an existing view,** select **All contacts.**
    c) In the **Name** section, in the **View Name** box type *<Your User Name> Grouped Contacts*
    d) Scroll down to the bottom of the page, next to **Group By,** select the **Expand** button.

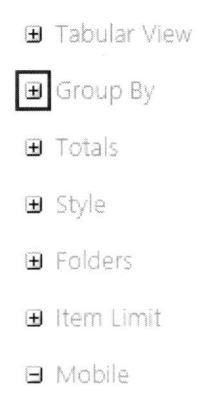

    ⊞ Tabular View
    ⊞ Group By
    ⊞ Totals
    ⊞ Style
    ⊞ Folders
    ⊞ Item Limit
    ⊟ Mobile

    e) In the **Group By** section, in the **First group by the column** drop-down list, select **State/Province**.
    f) Verify that **Show groups in ascending order** is selected.
    g) In the **Then group by the column** drop-down list, select **City**.

h) Under **By default, show groupings,** verify the **Collapsed** is selected.

```
Group By
Select up to two columns to determine what type of group
and subgroup the items in the view will be displayed in. Learn
about grouping items.

                                          First group by the column:
                                          [ State/Province            v ]

                                          (•)  Show groups in ascending order
                                               (A, B, C, or 1, 2, 3)

                                          ( )  Show groups in descending order
                                               (C, B, A, or 3, 2, 1)

                                          Then group by the column:
                                          [ City                      v ]

                                          (•)  Show groups in ascending order
                                               (A, B, C, or 1, 2, 3)

                                          ( )  Show groups in descending order
                                               (C, B, A, or 3, 2, 1)

                                          By default, show groupings:
                                          (•) Collapsed  ( ) Expanded

                                          Number of groups to display per page:
                                          [ 30 ]
```

i) At the bottom of the page, select **OK**.

j) On the **Orange Contacts** page, expand **State/Province: KS,** then expand **City: Topeka** to view **Kansas** contacts.

k) On the **Orange Contacts** page, expand **State/Province: NY,** then expand **City: Westchester** to view **New York** contacts.

l) In the **Quick Launch** area, select **Project Orange Home**.

Summary

In this lesson, you learned about SharePoint lists, the types of lists available, and list components, including columns, and other components that make up list views. You added items to lists, modified items in lists, created and modified list views, and created views that were filtered and grouped based on criteria you specified.

In your work environment, how could you use list views to make your job easier?

What types of SharePoint lists would your team find useful?

> **Note:** Check your LogicalCHOICE Course screen for opportunities to interact with your classmates, peers, and the larger LogicalCHOICE online community about the topics covered in this course or other topics you are interested in. From the Course screen you can also access available resources for a more continuous learning experience.

4 Configuring Your SharePoint Profile

Lesson Time: 1 hour

Lesson Objectives

In this lesson, you will:

- Update your SharePoint profile.

- Share, tag, and follow content in SharePoint, and see how that information is rolled up in your personal site.

- Create a blog and manage blog categories, posts, and comments.

Lesson Introduction

SharePoint® is a tool for collaboration, and sharing content and information with libraries and lists is central to collaboration. However, to get the most out of SharePoint you should take advantage of the personal collaboration features that are built-in. In this lesson, you will learn about your SharePoint profile. In this lesson, you will also learn about the personal collaboration and social networking features built-in to SharePoint.

Many of the features that make SharePoint a great tool for team collaboration, also make it a great tool for personal collaboration. The fact that SharePoint is a central location that is frequently visited by your colleagues, makes it an excellent place for you to share not only documents and files, but also personal information about yourself. By utilizing the personal collaboration and social networking feature of SharePoint, you can build relationships, spot trends, advance interests, and work more effectively with your team members and colleagues.

TOPIC A

Update and Share Your Profile Information

The first step in successfully using the personal collaboration and social networking features in SharePoint is to update your profile information so that your colleagues will know something about you. In this topic, you will update your SharePoint profile.

SharePoint Profile Information

Your *SharePoint Profile* stores information about you. It is associated with your user login and allows other users to learn about you. Your profile contains basic information such as your name, department, title, and manager, provides contact information such as email address, phone numbers, and address, and allows you to share more about your past projects, skills, schools, interests, and other personal data. You can also upload a picture of yourself to further personalize your profile. Filling out your profile information lets the people you collaborate with get to know you better, and gives them a better picture of your professional skills and experience.

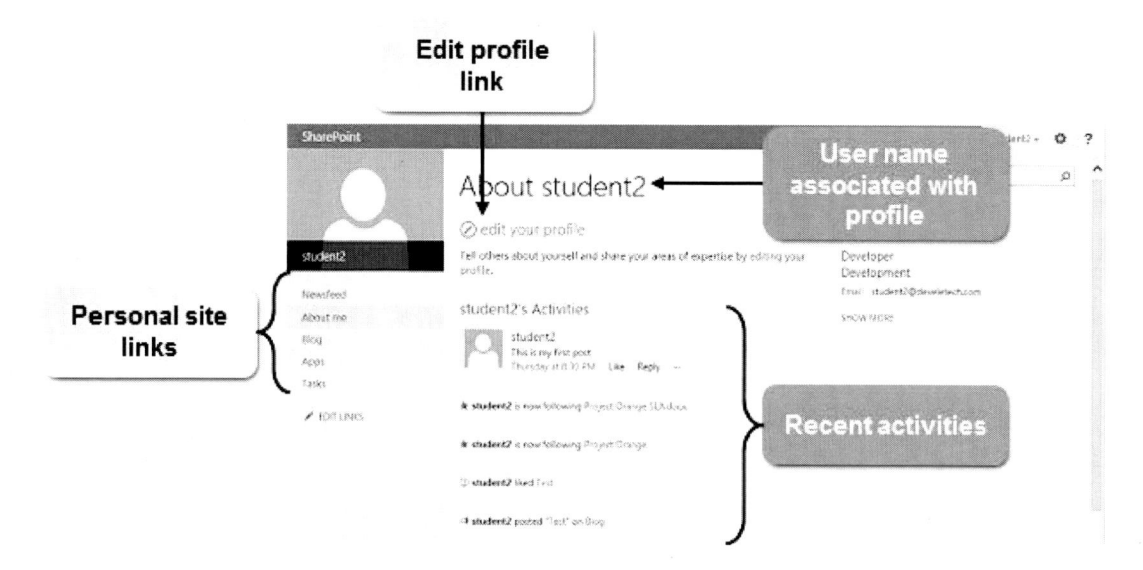

Figure 4-1: Your SharePoint profile.

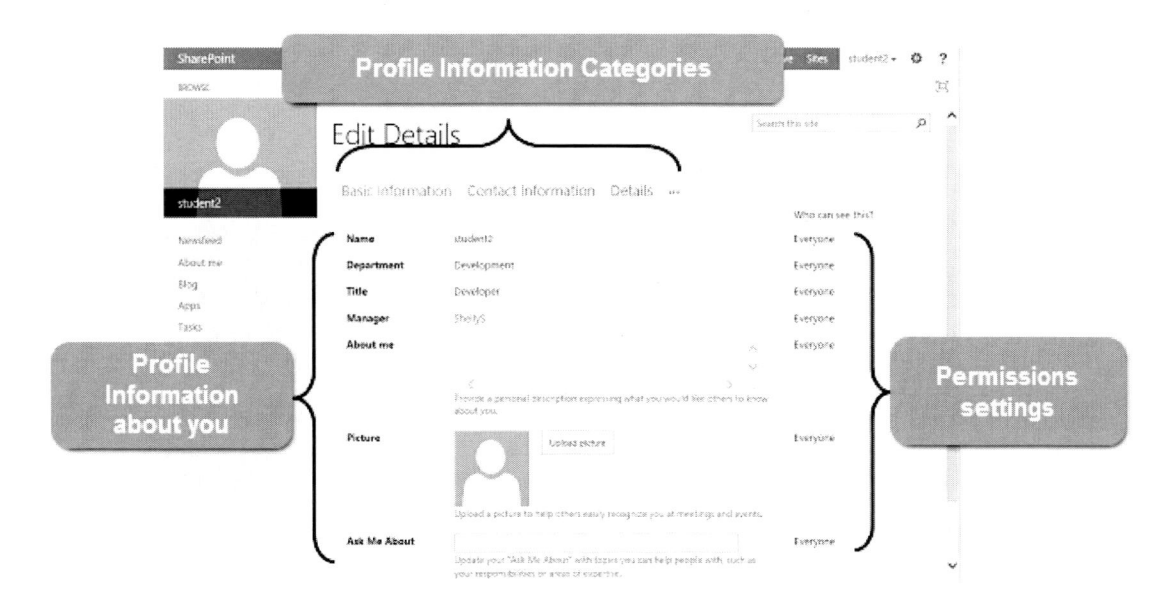

Figure 4-2: Editing your SharePoint profile.

Sources of Profile Information

Much of the basic and contact information in your profile may come from Active Directory® or other external sources depending on how SharePoint is configured. It is common for SharePoint to have a connection with Active Directory and populate information such as Name, Department, Title, and contact information from Active Directory. Some of the information populated from these external sources cannot be edited in the profile edit page.

Profile Access Permissions

When you edit your SharePoint profile, you can choose who to share certain profile information with. Much of the basic information is automatically shared with everyone because it often comes from Active Directory or some other directory source and is generally available within the company anyway. You have the option to control other information, such as home phone, and items on the details page of your profile, such as skills, birthday, and interests. When editing your profile, you can see the permissions associated with each information item. For the items to which you control permissions, you can select set the permission to **Only Me,** essentially turning the feed off for that item, or set it to **Everyone,** allowing all SharePoint users to see it.

> Access the Checklist tile on your CHOICE Course screen for reference information and job aids on How to Update and Share Your SharePoint Profile.

ACTIVITY 4-1
Updating and Sharing Your SharePoint Profile

Before You Begin

You should be logged onto the classroom SharePoint site, and your browser should have the Project Orange home page open.

Scenario

In order to get the most out of SharePoint, you should update your profile with personal information so that your coworkers can learn more about you personally and professionally. In this activity, you will update your SharePoint profile information.

1. Access your profile.
   a) In **SharePoint**, in the header, select the drop-down arrow next to **<Your User Name>** and then select **About Me**.

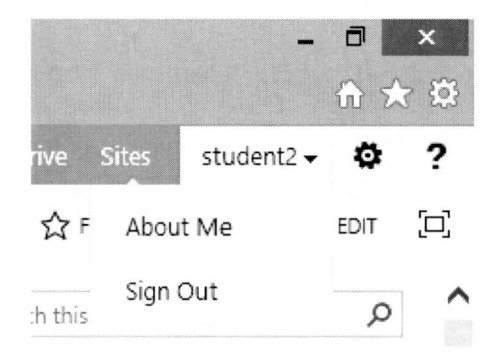

   b) Observe the **About <Your User Name>** page and the links on the left of the page.

   > **Note:** The left navigation area lets you easily navigate between your Newsfeed, profile, blog, apps and tasks.

   c) Select **edit your profile**.

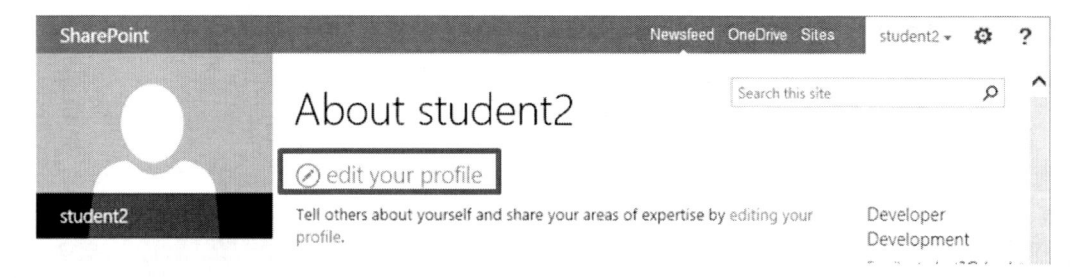

   d) On the **Edit Details** page, in the **Name** box, verify your account name is correct.

2. Update basic profile information.

a) In the **About Me** box, type a few sentences to describe yourself.

> Basic Information   Contact Information   Details   ...
>
> **Name**   student2
>
> **About me**   Know more about me. Now you know.
>
> Provide a personal description expressing what you would like others to know about you.

> **Note:** If you wanted to add a picture of yourself, you would select the picture graphic at the top left side of the page.

b) In the **Ask Me About** box, type *Quality Assurance testing and review on large projects*
c) Under **Who can see this,** observe the settings.

> **Note:** You cannot modify the **Who can see this** setting for some of your profile information that is publicly available from your directory service.

3. Update contact information for your profile.
   a) Below **Edit Details**, select **Contact Information.**

Edit Details

> Basic Information   Contact Information   Details   ...

   b) In the **Home Phone** box, enter a phone number.
   c) Below **Edit Details**, select **Details.**
   d) In the **Skills** box, type *Quality Assurance Testing*
   e) In the **Schools** box, type a school of your choice.
   f) In the **Interests** box, type a few personal interests.
   g) Select **Save all and close.**
   h) A message box appears telling you that the changes may take a while to take effect, select **OK**.

TOPIC B

Share and Follow SharePoint Content

The next step in using SharePoint personal collaboration and social networking features is to learn how your personal sites are organized and how they are designed to be used. In this topic, you will review your personal sites, then tag and follow content and use other social networking features to see your personal sites can be personal collaboration and social networking hubs.

Personal Sites as a Collaboration Space

In SharePoint, *personal sites,* or MySites, are personal collaboration spaces, that allow you to quickly access sites, documents, and people of interest, and to share your own documents for collaboration. Your personal site is associated with your login account and is made up of three hub pages. The **Newsfeed** provides a place for you to post status updates and have online conversations, and also provides a unified view of the people you're following. Your OneDrive® provides you a place to store and share your files and allows you to track documents you're following. Your **Sites** rolls up the sites that you're following. You can share documents and other items from your MySite with your colleagues. Your **Newsfeed, OneDrive,** and **Sites** are accessed from the header in SharePoint, making them easy to get to from anywhere.

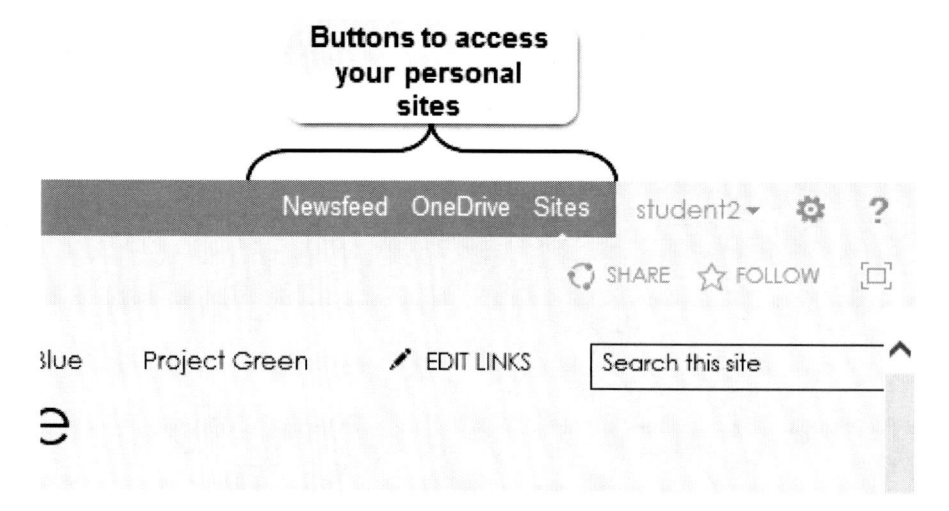

Figure 4-3: Personal site access.

> **Note:** In a previous lesson, you opened your **Newsfeed, OneDrive,** and **Sites.** These pages are created and configured the first time they are opened.

Following in SharePoint

In SharePoint 2013, the best way to stay current on items or people you are interested in is to follow them. You can follow almost anything in SharePoint including entire sites, libraries, and lists, or you can be more specific and follow individual documents, items, contacts, events, tags, and people. *Following* is simple; open the item you wish to follow and select **FOLLOW** from the ribbon. Items you're following are tracked on the appropriate page in your MySite. For example, sites you're following are tracked on your **Sites** page, while documents you follow are tracked on your **OneDrive.**

Figure 4-4: The FOLLOW button.

Tags and Tagging in SharePoint

Tagging means to associate keywords or phrases with information to allow people to find that information when they search using those familiar terms. In SharePoint you can tag sites, documents, and posts to make it easy for other people to find them, or to make it easier to track content and find it again later. SharePoint has multiple areas where tags can be assigned, and subtle differences in the tagging interaction and tag behavior, as explained in the table.

Where the Tag is Used	Type of Tag	Tagging Behavior
Documents and Sites (through the **Tags and Notes** window)	Keyword Tag	Users enter keywords through the **Tags and Notes** window. AutoComplete will suggest keywords from the list of Enterprise Keywords and hashtags in SharePoint. Depending on SharePoint configuration, tags entered this way may or may not be tracked in **Newsfeed**.
Newsfeed and Community Site posts	Hashtag	Users enter hashtags in posts to assign keywords and categories to their posts. Users may also follow or find related content for hashtags in other posts.

Tags Tracked in Your Newsfeed

SharePoint rolls up information about social tags in your **Newsfeed**. By default, only hashtags are considered social tags by SharePoint unless the site owner or administrator has enabled the **Save metadata on this list as social tags** box on the configuration settings for the library or site.

Hashtags

Hashtags are a new form of tag available in SharePoint 2013. Often written as #tag, and pronounced hashtag, these tags are meant to be used the same way tags are used on social networks. You can include a hashtag in a post on your Newsfeed or in a community site to assign keywords that categorize the posts. You create a hashtag by typing a # in front of any word (leaving out spaces). For example, typing #engineering would create that hashtag. SharePoint will identify the term as a hashtag. When hashtags are included in posts, you can choose to follow the hashtag, to track documents or conversations on the same topic, and select hashtags to find related content. You can select tags to follow as part of your Newsfeed.

Newsfeed

The *Newsfeed* is one of the hub pages that is part of each user's personal site, or MySite. Your Newsfeed provides you with a personal status form, like many social network sites, that you can share with your team, members of sites you're following, or everyone. You can post status updates. You and others with access can reply to posts to have conversations. Your Newsfeed also rolls social networking style updates delivered as separate sections. As you start using SharePoint, following people, and collaborating via forums and posts, you should visit your Newsfeed often to get updates as to the most recent changes on the things that you're interested in.

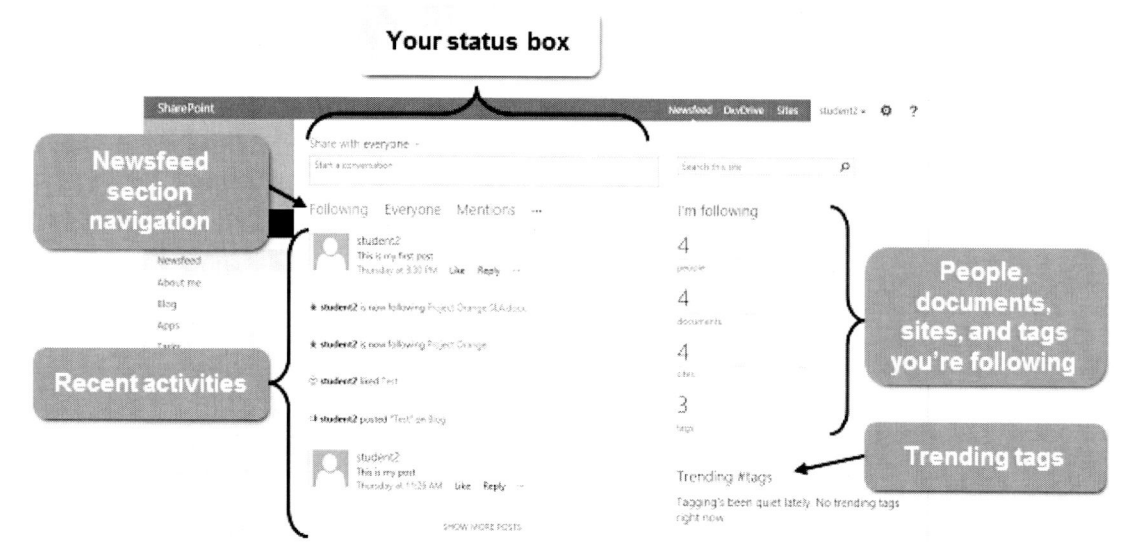

Figure 4-5: The Newsfeed.

Newsfeed Section	Description
Following	Shows updates for sites, documents, people and tags that you're following.
Everyone	Shows all conversations started and shared with everyone in the organization.
Mentions	Lists posts that you've been mentioned in with the @ symbol followed by your user name.
Activities	Shows your current activities similar to the **About Me** page.
Likes	Lists posts that you've "liked."

Mentions

SharePoint users can mention other users by typing an @ symbol followed by the users name (for example @jsmith). You can mention someone to bring a post to their attention because the mention will be rolled up on their Newsfeed.

OneDrive Pro

Your *OneDrive Pro* is a place for you to create, store, and organize your personal documents and files. You might use this in place for storing documents on your local machine, or on a file share. The documents are stored securely in SharePoint and are kept private until you decide to share them. You can share documents with colleagues, and control whether they can view or edit documents and set alerts to be informed if any changes are made. You can access the documents and files in OneDrive from anywhere that you can access SharePoint, and from any device that can access

SharePoint. You can also synchronize your OneDrive to a folder on your local system or other mobile devices so that you can work offline.

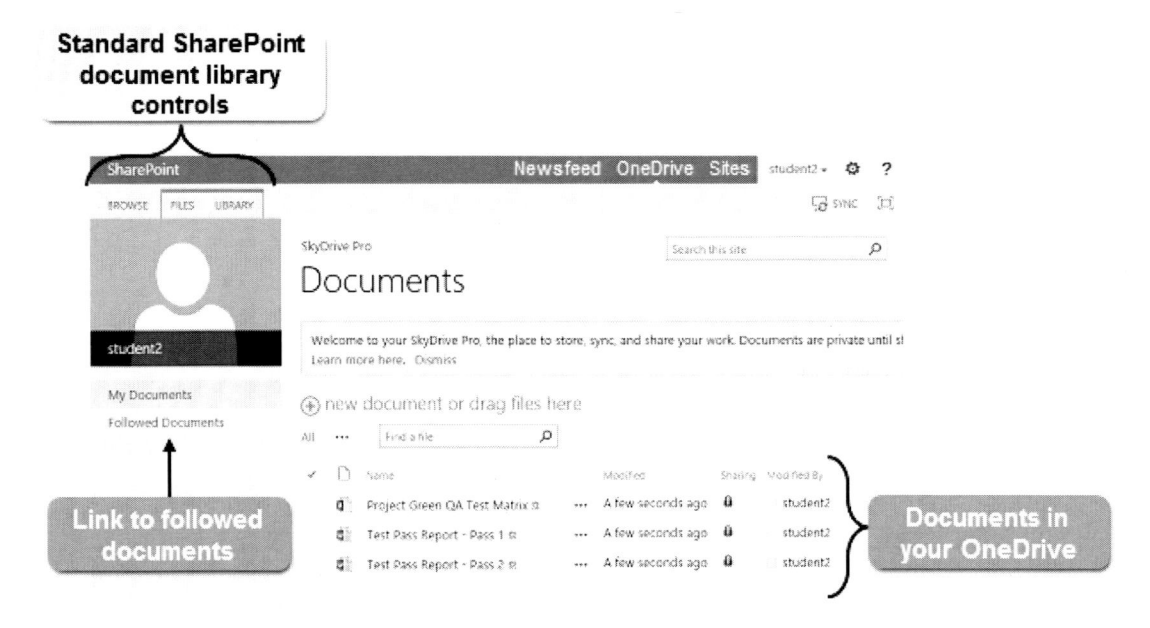

Figure 4-6: OneDrive.

OneDrive File Storage Location

If you have on-premises SharePoint, files uploaded to your OneDrive are stored on the SharePoint server or server farm. If you have SharePoint Online or Office 365™ with SharePoint, your files are stored in the cloud with your SharePoint storage.

Sites

Your personal **Sites** page allows you to create your own team sites if your site administrators have allowed it. It also lists all the sites you're following so that you can quickly navigate to any of those sites from your personal **Sites** page. Site administrators can also promote specific sites on your **Sites** page to draw your attention to them.

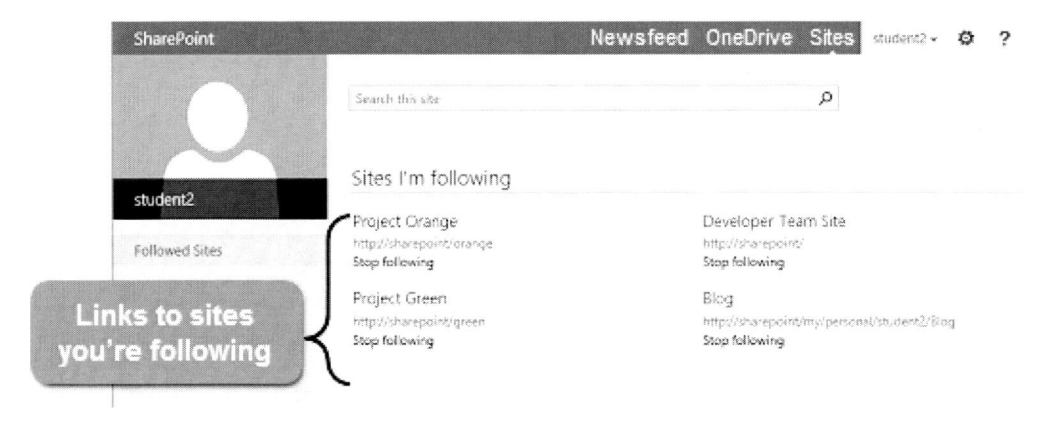

Figure 4-7: The Sites page.

> Access the Checklist tile on your CHOICE Course screen for reference information and job aids on How to Share and Follow Content.

ACTIVITY 4-2
Sharing and Following Content

Before You Begin
You should be logged into the classroom SharePoint site, and your browser should have your SharePoint profile page open.

Scenario
Your supervisor has encouraged you and the rest of her team to take advantage of the social networking features of SharePoint to collaborate more effectively. To accomplish this, you are going to review your MySite including your Newsfeed, OneDrive and Sites. You are going to go through the Developer Team site and project sites and tag and follow content that you wish to stay current on. You will then see how this information is rolled up in your MySite.

---

1. Review your **Newsfeed, OneDrive** and **Sites**.
   a) In **SharePoint,** in the header bar, select **Newsfeed.**
   b) Observe the **Newsfeed** page.

2. Observe the instructor-led portion of Newsfeed, OneDrive, and Sites.
   a) Under the **Start a conversation** box, show the **Following, Everyone,** and **Mentions** links.
   b) Under the **Start a conversation** box, to the right of **Mentions**, select the **Additional options** button

   ...

   to show additional options of **Activities** and **Likes.**
   c) Show the **I'm following** section on the right side of the page.

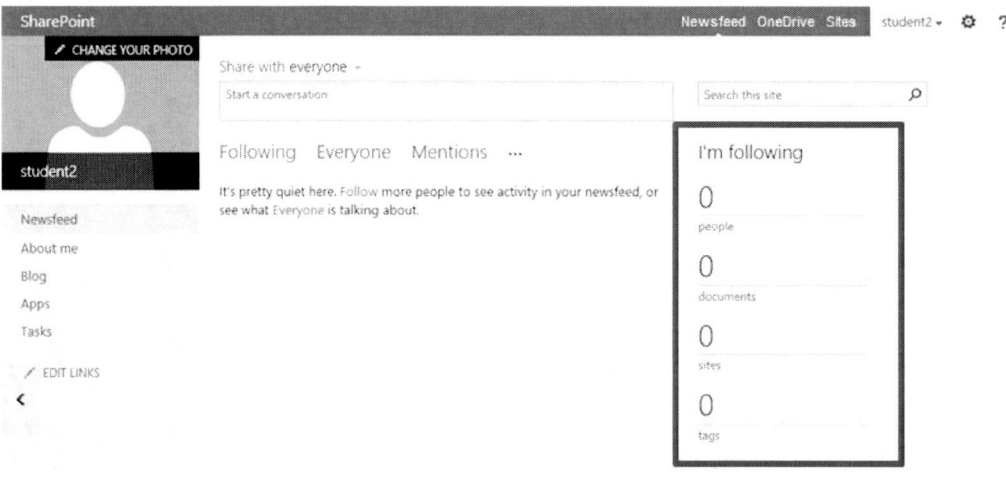

   d) In the header bar, select **OneDrive.**
   e) Observe your **OneDrive** page.
   f) In the header bar, select **Sites.**

g) Observe your **Sites** page.

3. Create a Word document in OneDrive.
    a) In the header bar, select **OneDrive.**
    b) On the **Documents** page, select **new document,** and in the **Create a new file** menu, select **Word document.**

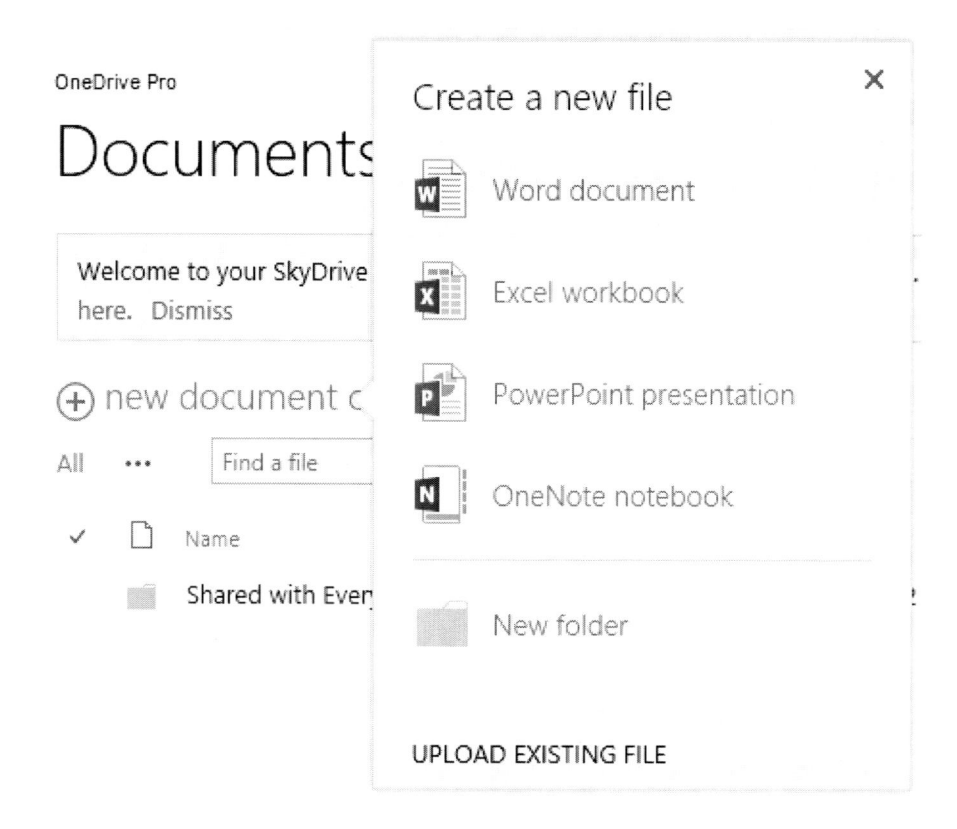

    c) In the **Create a new document** dialog box, in the **Document Name** box, type *<Your User Name> Shared document* and select **OK.**
    d) The new document opens in **Microsoft Word Web App.** In the body of the document type, *My shared document.*

e) On the **Quick Access** toolbar, select **Save**. Close **Microsoft Word Web App**.

> **Note:** Be careful in the next step to close the Word Web App, do not select the red X and close your browser.

> **Note:** You should be back in your OneDrive, if you are not, in the header select **OneDrive** to return to your OneDrive.

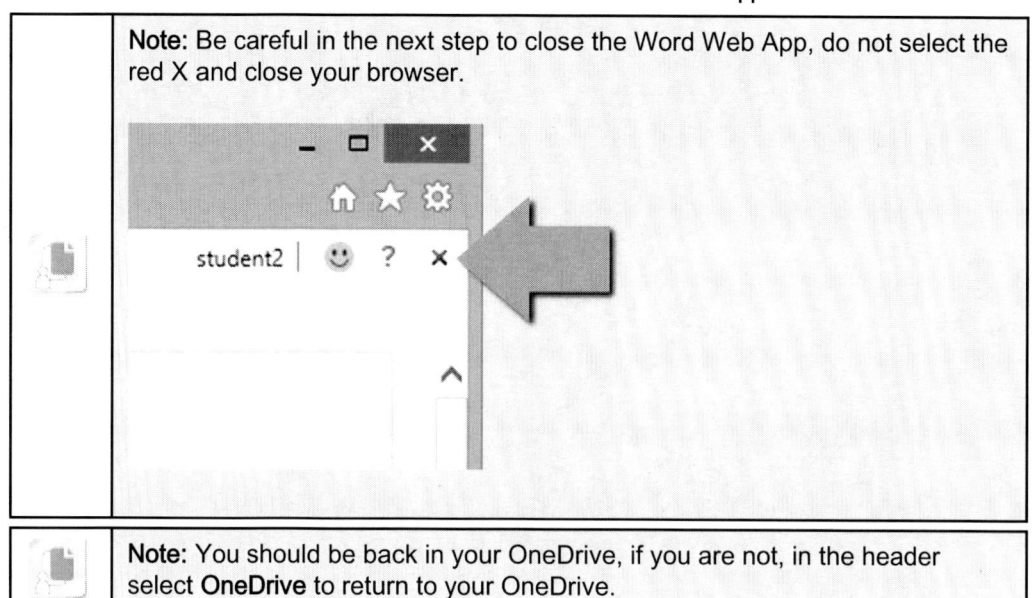

f) On the **Documents** page, observe the new document.

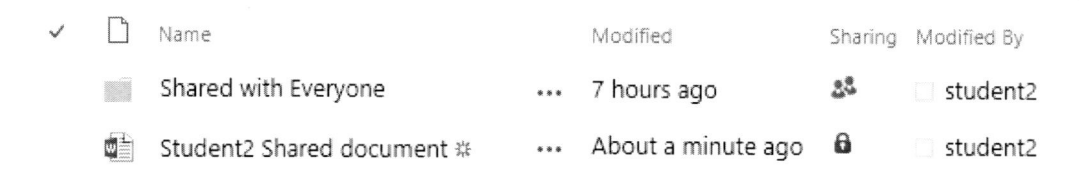

✓	Name		Modified	Sharing	Modified By
	Shared with Everyone	...	7 hours ago	👥	student2
	Student2 Shared document	...	About a minute ago	🔒	student2

4. Create an Excel workbook in OneDrive.
   a) Select **new document**, and in the **Create a new file** menu, select **Excel workbook**.
   b) In the **Create a new document** dialog box, in the **Document Name** box, type *<Your User Name> Shared spreadsheet* and select **OK**.
   c) The new document opens in **Microsoft Excel Web App**. In cell **A1** type *My shared spreadsheet*.
   d) On the ribbon, select the **FILE** tab, then select **Save As**.
   e) On the **Save As** page, select **Save As** to save a copy in the same OneDrive folder.
   f) In the **Save As** dialog box, check the **Overwrite existing files** check box, and select **Save**.

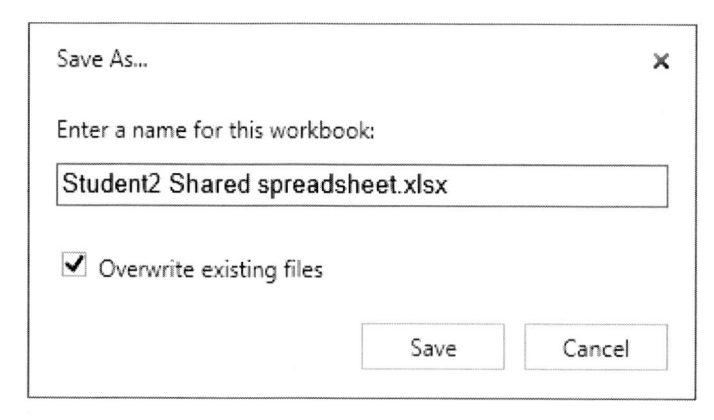

   g) Close **Microsoft Excel Web App**.

h) On the **Documents** page, observe the spreadsheet in your OneDrive.

	Name	Modified	Sharing	Modified By
	Shared with Everyone	... 7 hours ago	👥	student2
	Student2 Shared document	... 12 minutes ago	🔒	student2
	Student2 Shared spreadsheet	... 6 minutes ago	🔒	student2

5. Follow SharePoint sites.
   a) In your web browser, in the **Address box** type *http://sharepoint* and press **Enter**.
   b) On the ribbon, select **FOLLOW**.

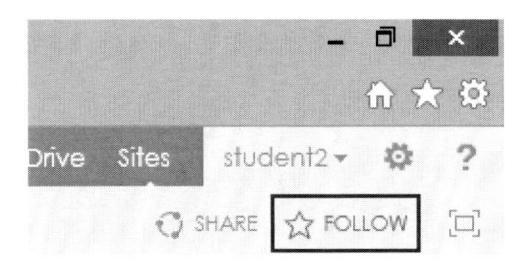

   c) Observe the message that appears in the upper-right portion of the page.

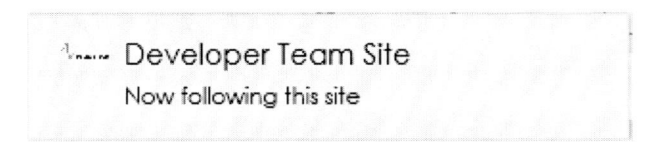

   > Developer Team Site
   > Now following this site

   d) In the **Quick Launch** area, under **Subsites**, select **Project Orange**.
   e) On the **Project Orange** page, select **Orange Documents**.
   f) On the ribbon, select **FOLLOW**.
   g) Observe the message that appears in the upper-right portion of the page.

   > Project Orange
   > Now following this site

6. Follow documents in SharePoint.
   a) In the **Top Links** bar, select **Developer Team Site**.
   b) In the **Quick Launch** area, select **Team Documents**.
   c) Next to **C++ and C Sharp development standards,** select the **Open Menu** button.
   d) In the preview window, select **FOLLOW**.

e) Observe the message that appears in the upper-right portion of the page.

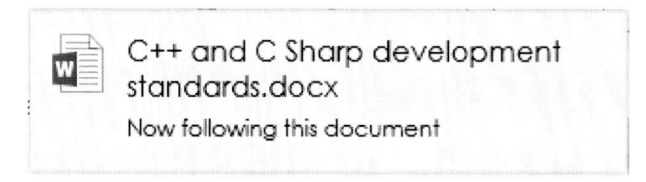

> C++ and C Sharp development standards.docx
> Now following this document

7. Create and assign tags.
    a) If necessary, on the **Team Documents** page, to the left of the **C++ and C Sharp development standards** document, select the check box to select that document.

    > **Note:** This document may already be selected as part of the previous **FOLLOW** command.

    b) Observe the highlighted check mark next to the document.

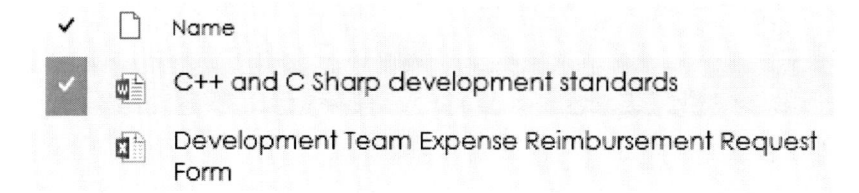

✓		Name
✓	📄	C++ and C Sharp development standards
	📄	Development Team Expense Reimbursement Request Form

    c) On the ribbon, select the **FILES** tab, then in the **Tags and Notes** group, select **Tags & Notes**.
    d) In the **Tags and Note Board** window, select the **Note Board** tab. In the box type *Good procedures for working on different portions of the code base simultaneously.*
    e) Select **Post**.
    f) Select the **Tags** tab.
    g) In the **My Tags** box, type *#<YourUserName>Good4ProjectOrange*

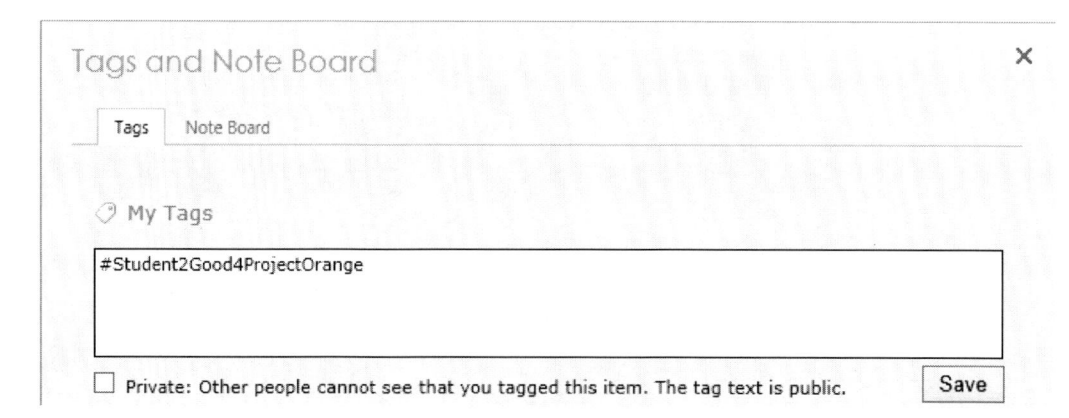

    Tags and Note Board

    Tags | Note Board

    My Tags

    #Student2Good4ProjectOrange

    ☐ Private: Other people cannot see that you tagged this item. The tag text is public.   [Save]

    > **Note:** You have to click in the upper-left side of the tags box to activate the cursor. Remember that there should be no spaces in hashtags.

    h) Select **Save**.

8. Access the tag profile to follow the tag.

a) Under **Suggested Tags,** select **#<YourUserName>Good4ProjectOrange.**

> Suggested Tags
> #Student2Good4Projec...

b) Under **#<YourUserName>Good4ProjectOrange** select **Go to Tag Profile for #<YourUserName>Good4ProjectOrange.**

> Suggested Tags
> #Student2Good4Projec...
> Go to Tag Profile for #Student2Good4ProjectOrange

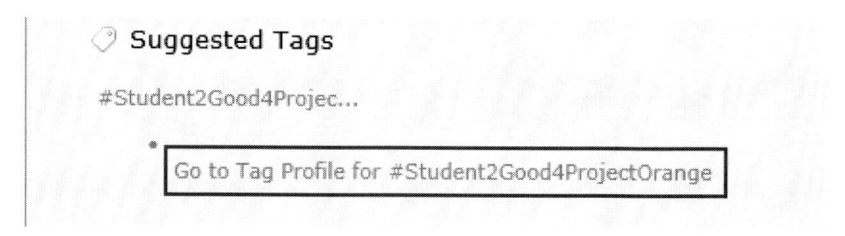

c) On the **Tag Profile > #<YourUserName>Good4ProjectOrange** page, select **Follow this tag in My Newsfeed.**

Tag Profile > #Student2Good4ProjectOrange

Tag Profile: #Student2Good4ProjectOrange

Found in: Keywords

Get Connected
- Follow this tag in My Newsfeed
- Add to "Ask Me About" in My Profile
- View people who are following this tag

Tagged Items

View: All | Popular within last 60 days
There are no available items tagged with '#Student2Good4ProjectOrange.'
To find content related to '#Student2Good4ProjectOrange' in search, please click here.

Note Board

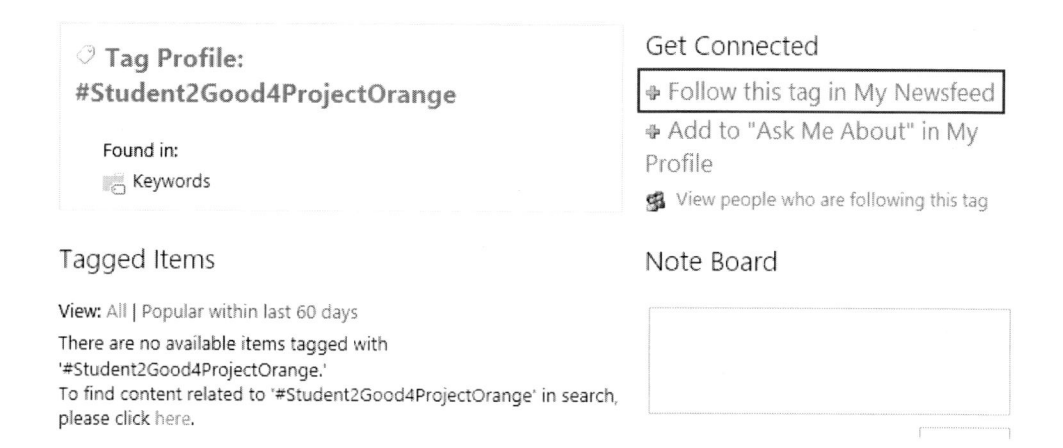

9. Add tags to other documents.
   a) In your web browser, select **Back,** then select **Back** again to return to the **Team Documents** page.
   b) On the **Team Documents** page, to the left of the **Development Team On Call Escalation Procedures** document, select the check box to select the document.
   c) On the ribbon, select the **FILES** tab, then in the **Tags and Notes** group, select **Tags & Notes.**
   d) In the **Tags and Note Board** window, in the **My Tags** box, type *#<YourUserName>Administrative*
   e) Select **Save,** then close the window.
   f) On the **Team Documents** page, to the left of the **Development Team On Call Escalation Procedures** document, select the check box to deselect the document.
   g) On the **Team Documents** page, to the left of the **Development Team Travel Guidelines** document, select the check box to select the document.
   h) In the **FILES** tab, in the **Tags and Notes** group, select **Tags & Notes.**
   i) In the **Tags and Note Board** window, in the **My Tags** box, type *#<YourUserName>Travel*

j) Select **Save,** then close the window.

10. View people, sites, and documents you're following in your Newsfeed.
    a) In the header bar, select **Newsfeed.**
    b) Observe the sites and documents that you're following.

    I'm following

    0
    people

    1
    documents

    2
    sites

    0
    tags

    c) Under **I'm following,** select the number above **people.**
    d) Observe the **People I'm following** page.
    e) Select the **Back** button to return to your Newsfeed.
    f) Under **I'm following,** select the number above **documents.**
    g) Observe the **Docs I'm following** page.

    Docs I'm following

    C++ and C Sharp development standards
    http://sharepoint/Shared Documents/C++ and C...
    Stop following

    h) Select the **Back** button to return to your Newsfeed.
    i) Under **I'm following,** select the number above **sites.**
    j) Observe the **Sites I'm following** page.
    k) Select the **Back** button to return to your Newsfeed.

11. Observe tags that you're following in your Newsfeed.
    a) Under **I'm following,** select the number above **tags.**

b) On the **Edit Details** page, in the **Followed #Tags** box, type *#travel;#administrative*

Edit Details

Basic Information   Contact Information   Newsfeed Settings   ...

Followed #Tags   `#travel;#administrative`

Stay up-to-date on topics that interest you by following #tags. Posts with these #tags will show up in your newsfeed.

c) Observe the settings for **Email Notifications, People I follow,** and **Activities I want to share in my Newsfeed.**
d) Select **Save all and close.**

> **Note:** You may need to scroll down to see the **Save all and close** button.

e) You are prompted that your changes have been saved but may take some time to take effect, select **OK.**
f) On the **Newsfeed** page, under **I'm following,** observe the number of tags that you're following.

TOPIC C

Create a Blog

In addition to the other personal collaboration and social networking features provided by SharePoint, you can also create your personal blog to share your thoughts, experiences, and advance topics of interest. In this topic, you will create, post to, comment on, and manage your personal SharePoint blog.

Blogs

Blogs, the shortened term for web log, is an online log of discrete writings on topics that are of interest to the individual or group that is publishing the blog. In a professional organization, blogs can be used to document personal or professional experiences, or may provide behind-the-scenes insight to a project or team, or may share ideas or interests. Blogs often contain text, graphic images, and links to other blogs and resources on the Internet. SharePoint allows users to easily create a blog as part of their personal site. After you create a blog, you can post entries to your blog that others can see. Users can reply and like blog posts, and can follow blogs that they like.

> **Access the Checklist tile on your CHOICE Course screen for reference information and job aids on How to Manage and Post to Your Blog.**

ACTIVITY 4-3
Creating and Posting Entries to Your Blog

Before You Begin
You should be logged onto the classroom SharePoint site, and your browser should have your Newsfeed page open.

Scenario
Because quality control is one of your specialities, your supervisor has asked you to keep a blog about quality assurance for Project Orange as part of your SharePoint MySite. In this activity, you will create the blog, create your first blog post, share the blog with a colleague, comment on another coworker's blog, and manage comments on your own blog.

1. Create your blog.
    a) In the **Navigation** pane, select **Blog**. SharePoint will create your blog.

    > Newsfeed
    > About me
    > Blog
    > Apps
    > Tasks
    >
    > ✏ EDIT LINKS

    b) Observe the **Blog** page.

2. Configure blog categories.
    a) On the **Blog** page, observe the default categories.
    b) In the **Navigation** pane, under **Categories,** select **ADD CATEGORY.**
    c) In the **Categories→New Item** page, in the **Title** box, type *Quality Assurance Testing* and select **Save.**
    d) Verify that your new category appears under **Categories.**

    > Categories
    >   Events
    >   Ideas
    >   Opinions
    >   Quality Assurance Testing
    >   ADD CATEGORY

    e) Under **Blog tools,** select **Manage categories.**

f) On the **Categories** page, under **Categories,** next to **Events,** select the **Open Menu** button, and select **Delete Item.**

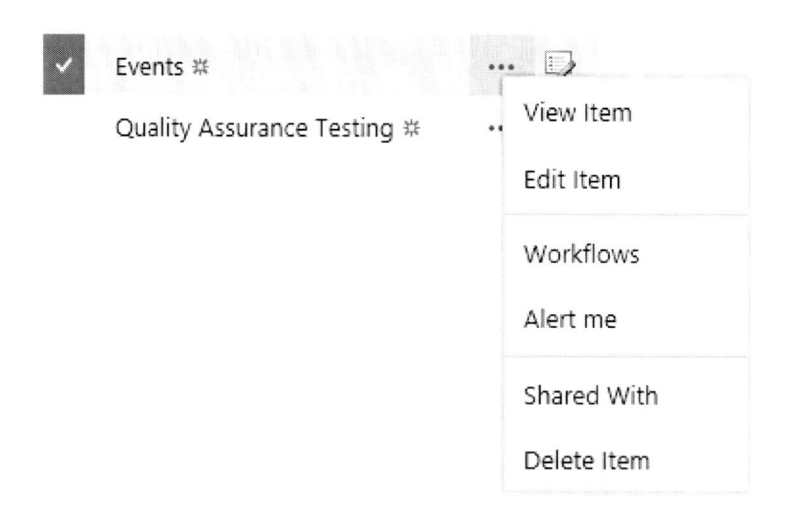

g) Select **OK** to confirm the deletion.
h) In the **Navigation** pane, select **Home.**

3. Create a blog post.
    a) On the **Blog** page, under **Blog tools** select **Create a post.**
    b) In the **Posts→New Item** page, in the **Title** box, type *Quality Assurance Testing Practices*
    c) In the **Body** box, type *This is the first in a series of good QA practices.*
    d) In the **FORMAT TEXT** ribbon, observe the text formatting options available.
    e) In the **Body** box, select the text you typed earlier.
    f) In the **FORMAT TEXT** ribbon, in the **Styles** group, in the **Styles** drop-down list, select **Emphasis.**

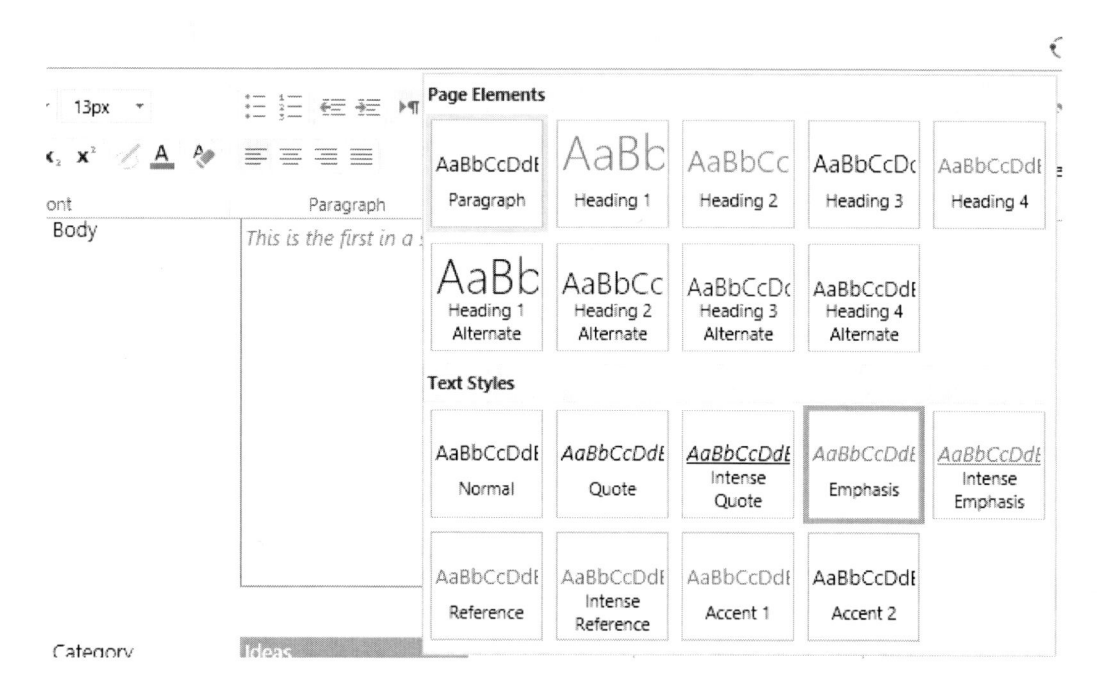

    g) In the **Category** box, select **Quality Assurance Testing** and select **Add.**

h) In the **Category** box, select **Opinions,** and select **Add.**

i) Select **Publish.**
j) Observe your new post.

4. Email a link to your post.
   a) Under your new post, select **Email a link.**

   b) A prompt appears asking you how you want to open this type of link, select **Outlook (desktop).**

   > **Note:** You may be prompted to allow this website to open a program on your computer, if so select allow.

   c) If you receive a certificate error, select **Yes.**

d) In the **Quality Assurance Testing Practices Message** Outlook window, in the **To** box, type the user name of a student partner, and select **Send**.

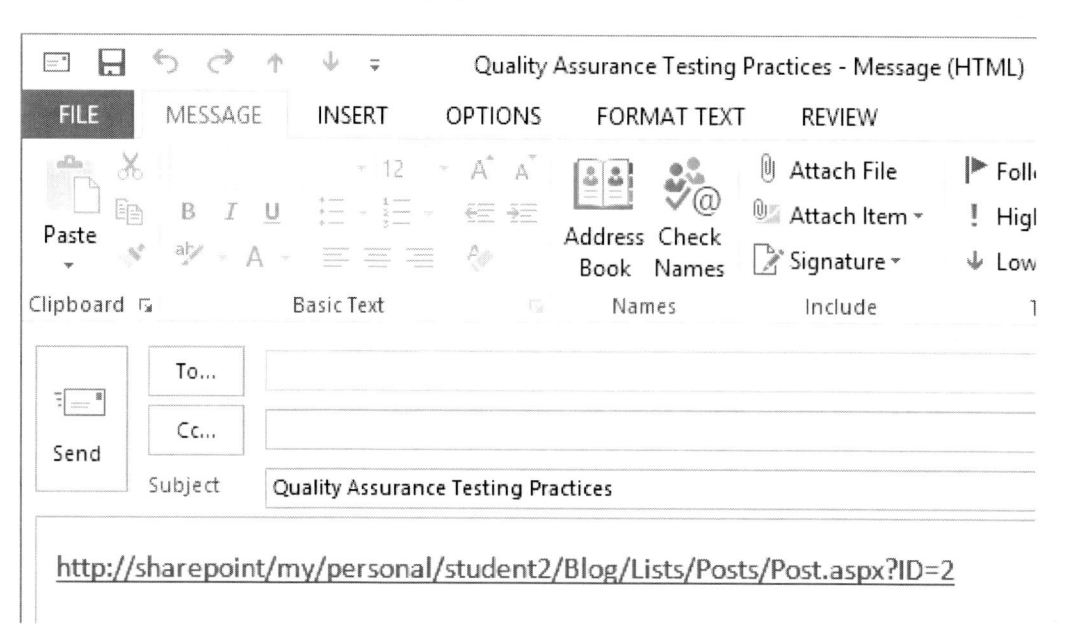

5. Comment on another person's blog post.
    a) Open **Microsoft Outlook**.

    > **Note:** You should have a new message from your partner learner.

    b) In **Microsoft Outlook,** select the message from your partner learner.
    c) Select the link inside the message to open the blog post.

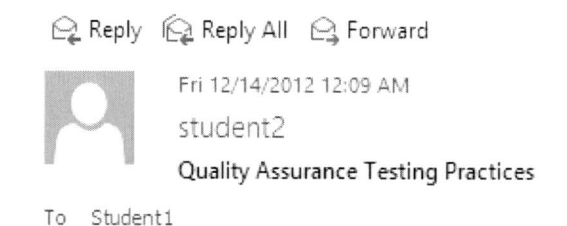

    > **Note:** You have just opened another browser window with another instance of the SharePoint Site

d) In the **Add a comment** box type *I think this is already covered in our standards documents* and select **Post**.

Blog

Quality Assurance Testing Practices
Thursday, December 13, 2012

This is the first in a series of good QA practices.

by student2 at 11:41 PM in Quality Assurance Testing, Opinions
Like   Comment   •••

0 comments
There are no comments for this post.

> I think this is already covered in our standards documents

[Post]

e) Observe your post in the blog.
f) In your web browser, close the current tab to close the additional SharePoint window that is open.

6. Manage comments on your blog.
    a) On the header bar, select **Newsfeed**.
    b) In the **Navigation pane**, select **Blog**.
    c) On the **Blog** page, under your **Quality Assurance Testing Practices** post, view the number of comments you have received.

d) Select the comment to open it.

Blog

Quality Assurance Testing Practices
Thursday, December 13, 2012

This is the first in a series of good QA practices.

by **student2** at 11:41 PM in Quality Assurance Testing, Opinions

| 1 comment | Like   Email a link   •••

e) Under **Blog tools**, select **Manage comments**.
f) On the **Comments** page, next to the new post select the **Open Menu** button, and select **Delete Item**.

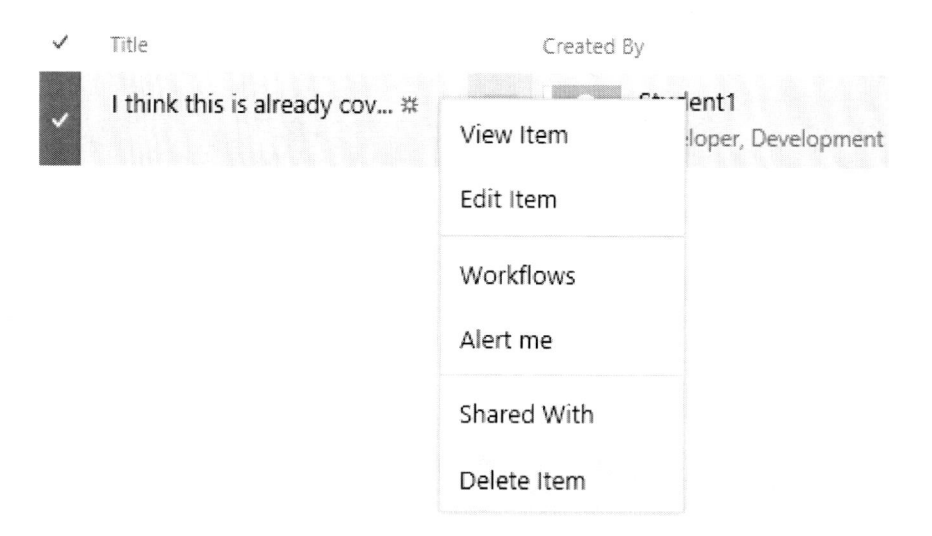

✓	Title	Created By
✓	I think this is already cov... ✱	student1

View Item

Edit Item

Workflows

Alert me

Shared With

Delete Item

g) Select **OK** to confirm the deletion.
h) In the Navigation pane, select **Home**.

i) On the **Blog** page, under your **Quality Assurance Testing Practice** post, select **Like**.

Blog

Quality Assurance Testing Practices
Thursday, December 13, 2012

This is the first in a series of good QA practices.

by **student2** at 11:41 PM in Quality Assurance Testing, Opinions
0 comments | Like | Email a link   •••

j) In your web browser, in the **Address** box, type *http://sharepoint* and press **Enter** to return to the **Developer Team Site** home page.

Summary

In this lesson, you learned about SharePoint profiles, and the three personal site hubs: your **Newsfeed, OneDrive,** and **Sites.** You also learned about following and tagging content in SharePoint. You updated your SharePoint profile to add information about yourself, then you followed sites and content and saw how that information was tracked on your Newsfeed. Finally you created a blog, posted to your blog, commented on another user's blog post, and managed blog categories and comments.

How would you follow content in your organization?

How do you think your organization could take advantage of SharePoint social collaboration features to improve productivity?

> **Note:** Check your LogicalCHOICE Course screen for opportunities to interact with your classmates, peers, and the larger LogicalCHOICE online community about the topics covered in this course or other topics you are interested in. From the Course screen you can also access available resources for a more continuous learning experience.

5 | Integrating with Microsoft Office

Lesson Time: 1 hour, 15 minutes

Lesson Objectives

In this lesson, you will:

- Access, create, save, and preview documents in SharePoint directly from Microsoft Office applications.

- Manage document versions through Office 2013.

- Synchronize content from SharePoint to Microsoft Outlook.

Lesson Introduction

Microsoft® Office applications are designed to integrate with SharePoint so that users can easily access documents stored in SharePoint®. There are a number of integration points between SharePoint and Microsoft Office applications. In this lesson, you will use integration features built into Microsoft Office applications to access documents in SharePoint, use document versioning features and document check-out features, and synchronize data from SharePoint to Microsoft® Outlook®.

The goal of these integration points is threefold. First, to ensure that accessing data in SharePoint is as easy as accessing data on the local client or any file server. Second, to service core collaboration features in Microsoft Office applications at times and in ways that make sense when working with documents. Third, to provide flexibility to individuals and allow them to work with the applications that they choose, and their documents in the way that works best for them. These integration points allow Microsoft Office applications and SharePoint to work very well when used together.

TOPIC A

Access and Save SharePoint Documents with Microsoft Office

At the most fundamental level, to work with documents in SharePoint, Microsoft Office applications have to see and be able to access the documents and content stored in SharePoint. In this topic, you will use Microsoft Office applications to access, create, update, and save documents in SharePoint.

SharePoint Integration with Office

Microsoft Office applications have historically integrated well with SharePoint. Office 2013 and SharePoint 2013 offer even tighter integration. The 2013 versions of both Office and SharePoint have been re-engineered with an emphasis on social networking features and access to cloud services. In addition, there are many enhancements that make accessing content and data stored in SharePoint easy and seamless from Office applications. The key integration points that make everyday interaction between Office and SharePoint easier are listed in the table.

Integration	Description
Easy access from Office apps	You can easily open and save content in SharePoint directly from your Office applications; you don't have to open the content in SharePoint. You can add shortcuts to your favorite SharePoint libraries directly to your Office applications.
Offline File Sync	Both Office and SharePoint support synchronization of files to OneDrive® for offline use. This is covered in more detail in a later lesson.
SharePoint versioning and check-out notification	Office applications are version and check-out aware and will notify you if you are opening a document in one of those states. Office applications will provide you with all SharePoint options for working with those features effectively.
Sync to Outlook	You can synchronize SharePoint libraries and lists with Microsoft® Outlook® so that you can view and work with documents, as well as list and calendar information directly from Outlook.

> Access the Checklist tile on your CHOICE Course screen for reference information and job aids on How to Work with Office 2013 Documents in SharePoint 2013.

ACTIVITY 5-1
Working with Office 2013 Documents in SharePoint 2013

Before You Begin
You should be logged onto the classroom SharePoint site, and your browser should have the SharePoint Developer Team site home page open.

Scenario
In your new job, your primary productivity tools will be Microsoft Office applications. Because SharePoint will be the primary collaboration tool, it's important that Office and SharePoint work well together. In this activity you will access documents and data stored in SharePoint from Microsoft Word, and save documents to SharePoint from Microsoft Word.

1. Access files in Office applications directly from SharePoint.
   a) In the **Quick Launch** area, select **Team Documents**.
   b) In the ribbon, select the **LIBRARY** tab, then in the **Connect and Export** group, select **Connect to Office**.

   > **Note:** Be sure to select the **Connect to Office** button, not the drop-down arrow.

   > **Note: Connect to Office** allows you to add shortcuts to the document library from your Office applications for ease of access.

   c) A prompt will appear asking if you trust the site; select **Yes**.
   d) Select **<Your User Name> Resume** to open the document in Microsoft Word Web App.
   e) Select **EDIT DOCUMENT**, and then select **Edit in Word**.

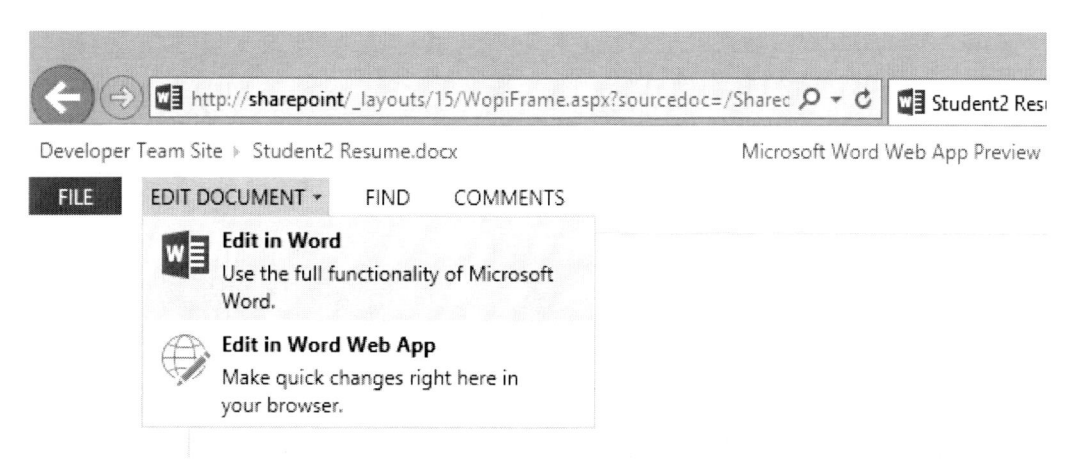

      f) The document opens in Microsoft Word.
      g) In the **READ-ONLY** warning prompt at the top of the document, select **Edit Document**.
      h) Type two lines of text in the document.

> **Note:** The specific text you type is not important. You just need to make an addition to the document.

2. Save files directly to SharePoint from Office applications.
    a) Select **FILE,** and then select **Save As.**

> **Note:** Your SharePoint site should be at the top of the list of locations to save the file.

    b) Under **SharePoint**, select the **Current Folder**.

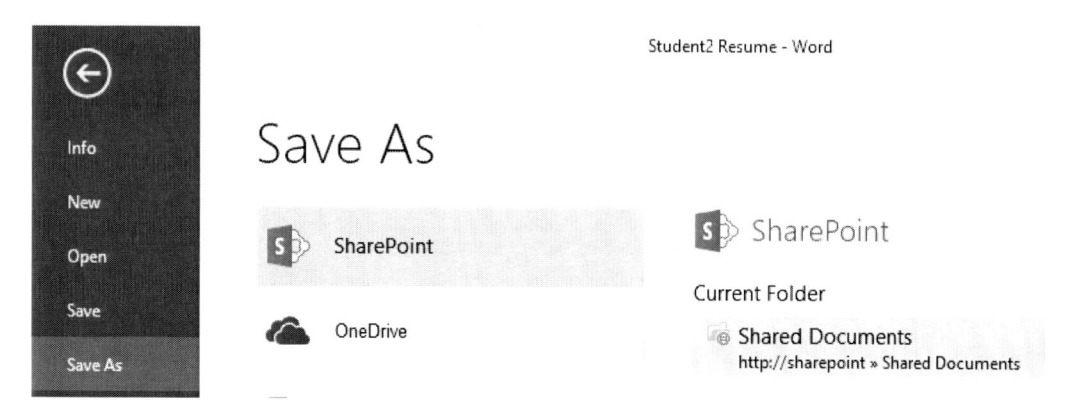

> **Note:** The name of the current folder should be **Shared Documents**.

    c) In the **Save As** dialog box, in the **File Name** box, type *<Your Use Name> Resume updated* and select **Save**.
    d) In Microsoft Word, select **FILE,** and then select **Open**.
    e) On the **Open** page, select **Recent Documents** if necessary, and select *<Your User Name> Resume*.
    f) Close all Word documents.
    g) In your web browser, close the **We're opening your document in Microsoft Word** dialog box.
    h) In your web browser, in the Word Web App select **FILE,** and then select **Exit** to close Microsoft Word Web App and return to the **Team Documents** library in SharePoint.

TOPIC B

Manage Document Versions through Office 2013

Microsoft Office applications allow you to easily take advantage of SharePoint content management features. In this topic, you will view version history, work with multiple versions of documents in Microsoft Office, check documents out and into SharePoint, and request deleted items be restored.

Document Versioning in SharePoint

SharePoint can store multiple iterations of documents and allow you to view, compare, and restore previous versions of documents if you need to. Document versioning must be turned on for each document library, and different document libraries can have different versioning settings. Accessing the version history for a document allows you to see the versions available, the dates each version was modified, and who made the modification, and the document size. There are three versioning settings in SharePoint Document Libraries.

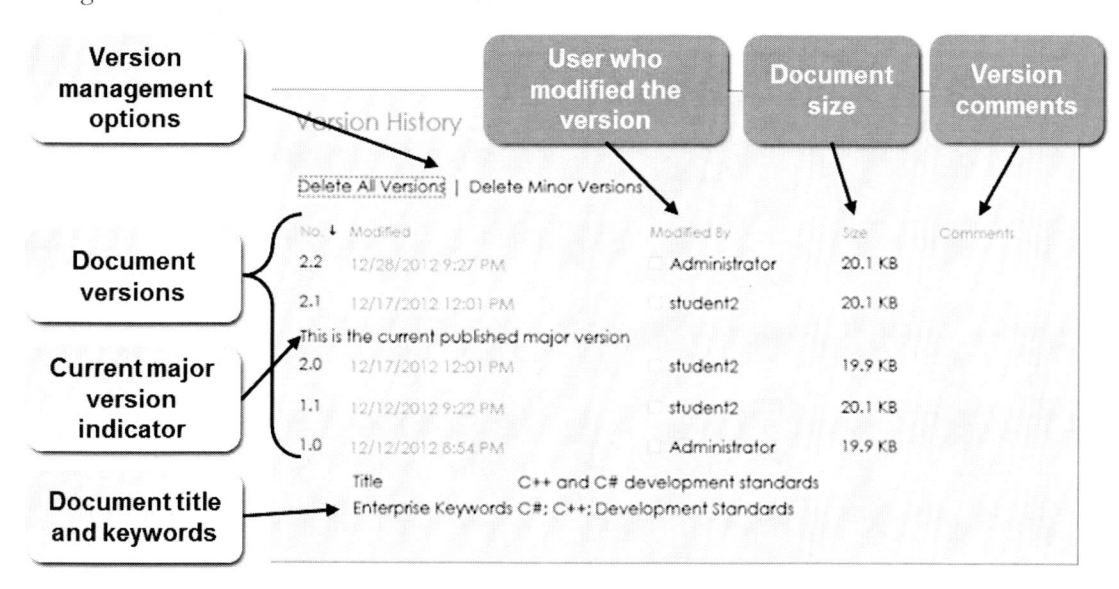

Figure 5-1: The version history in SharePoint.

Versioning Option	Description
No versioning	No earlier versions are saved, earlier versions of documents cannot be retrieved.
Create major versions	Numbered versions of documents are stored using a simple versioning scheme. Every time the document is saved, a new version is created.
Create major and minor (draft) versions	Numbered versions of documents are saved using major and minor versioning scheme. Versions ending in .0 are major versions. All users can read major versions and users with permissions can read minor versions. An example of where this might be useful is on a human resources site where employees might be allowed to see major versions, but only HR staff could see minor versions.

Working with Previous Versions in Office Applications

When you open a previous version of a document, the Office application warns you that the document is a previous version and gives you the option of comparing this version to the current version, or restoring this version to make it the current version.

Document Check In and Check Out in SharePoint

Site owners can require that documents are checked out of a SharePoint document library before they can be edited. When a document is checked out, it is locked for exclusive editing by that user. Other site users see a visual representation that the document is checked out. The user who has the document checked out can save changes without checking the document back in. Those changes are not visible to other users. After the document is checked back in, a new version of the document is created and becomes visible to other users. Microsoft Office applications integrate with SharePoint Check Out and Check In, allowing users to perform document check-out, undo check-outs, and check-ins from the Office applications.

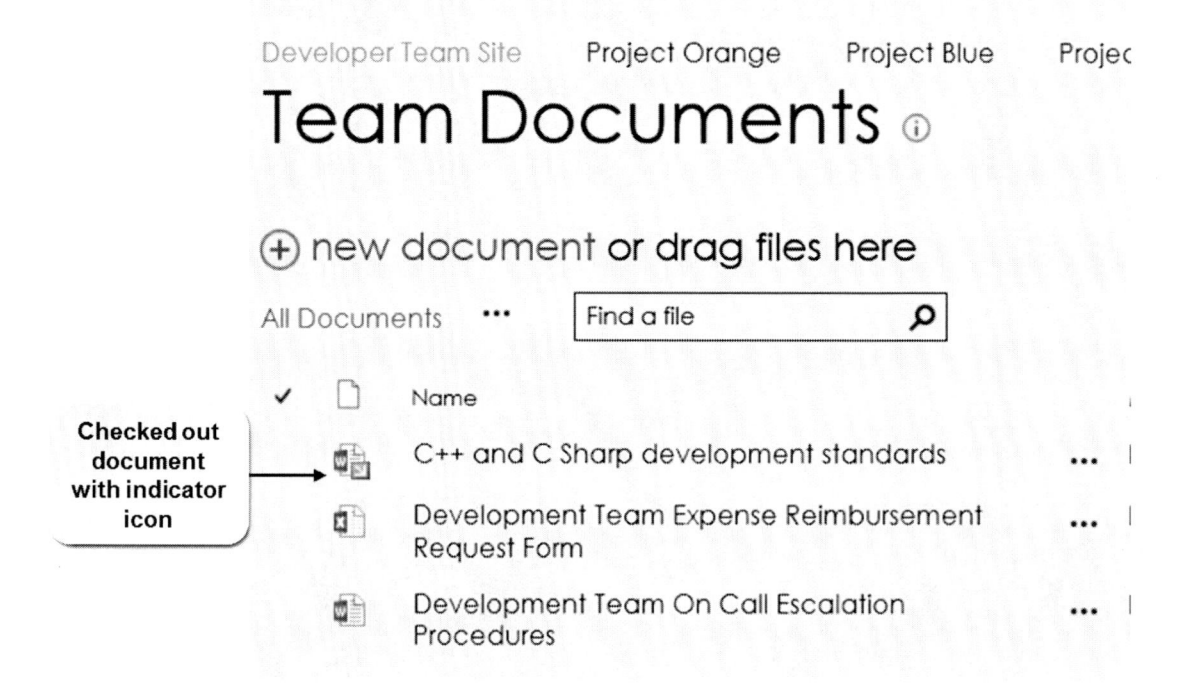

Figure 5-2: Checked out documents in SharePoint.

Benefits of Document Check Out

Requiring check-out has several benefits. The author has more control of when document versions are created because they can save iterative changes that are not visible to other users without checking the document back in. The author can also update the document properties to capture better metadata about each version.

Deleted Item Recovery in SharePoint

When users delete documents, list items, lists, folders, and files in SharePoint, they are sent to a recycle bin. This provides a safety net for users, allowing them to request recovery for items that were accidentally deleted. Items remain in the recycle bin for the Site Collection until permanently deleted. Users must contact the site owner, or an administrator with permissions to access the recycle bin for the Site Collection. The administrator can open the recycle bin and restore the item.

Note: Site owners have a scheduled time when the contents of the recycle bin will be permanently deleted. That timing is often related to when the site is backed up. Contact your site owner or administrator and ask them about the schedule so that you know the time frame in which you can request deleted item recovery.

Access the Checklist tile on your CHOICE Course screen for reference information and job aids on How to Manage Document Versions, Version Control, and Recovery in SharePoint.

ACTIVITY 5-2
Managing Document Versions, Version Control and Recovery in SharePoint

Before You Begin
You should be logged into the classroom SharePoint site, and your browser should have the Team Documents page open.

Scenario
As part of your job you will be working on a number specification documents that have multiple authors and contributors. To work effectively, your supervisor has asked you to familiarize yourself with SharePoint's version control, document check in and check out features, as well as document recovery options. In this activity, you will explore SharePoint document version features, view previous versions of documents, see versioning messages in Office applications, check documents out, view the results of attempting to work with a checked out document, and explore deleted item recovery.

1. Work with document versions in Office and SharePoint.
    a) On the **Team Documents** page, next to **C++ and C Sharp development standards,** select the **Open Menu** button, and on the document preview window select **Edit**.

    > **Note:** A dialog box may appear in the bottom-left portion of Microsoft Word informing you that other users are editing the document, and that you can view the list of other authors on the status bar and may provide options for viewing changes made by others. This is expected.

    b) In Microsoft Word, in the document body, under the existing text in the document, type *<Your User Name> Version 1.*
    c) Select **FILE,** and then select **Save.**
    d) In the document body, type *<Your User Name> Version 2.*
    e) Select **FILE,** and then select **Save.**
    f) Switch to your web browser and close the **C++ and C Sharp development standards** preview window.
    g) Observe the contents of the **Team Documents** library, and note that there is only one copy of the **C++ and C Sharp development standards** document in the library.

2. View document version history.

a) Next to **C++ and S Sharp development standards,** select the **Open Menu** button, in the document preview window, select the **Open Menu** button, and then select **Version History.**

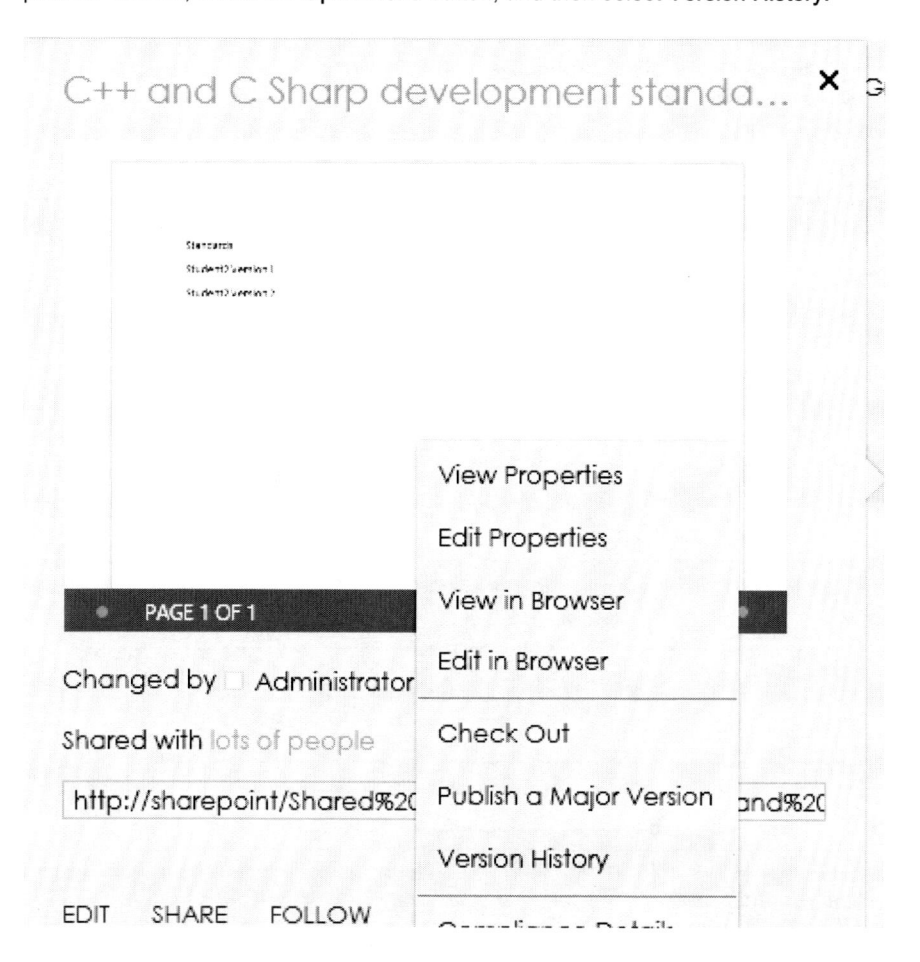

b) On the **Version History** window, review the versions on the SharePoint server.
c) Locate version **1.0** of the document, point to the date, and select the drop-down arrow next to the date of that version.
d) Observe the menu options available. Select the Version History window to close the menu.

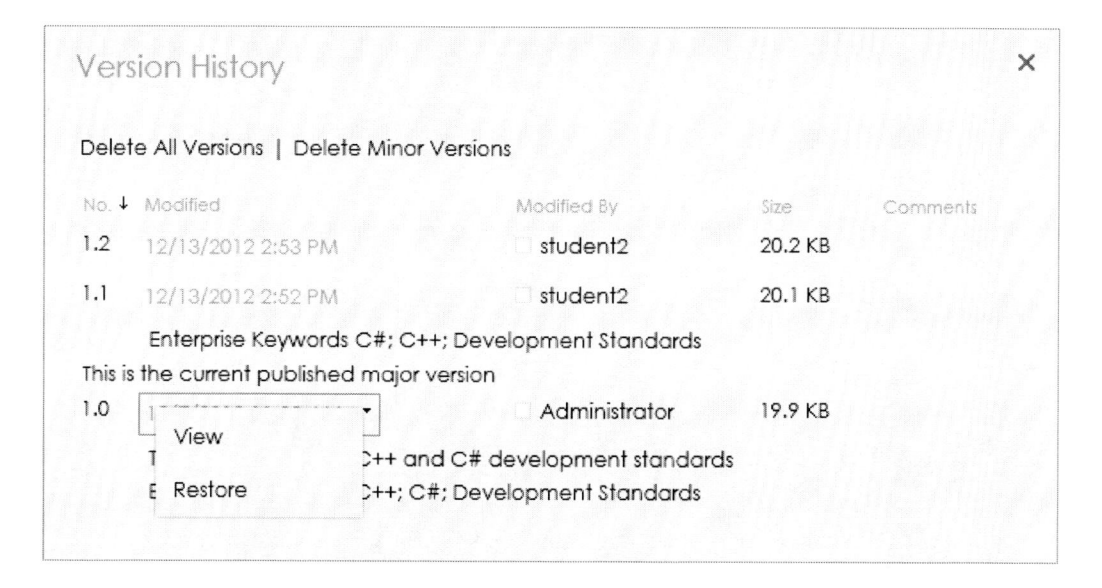

114 | Microsoft® SharePoint® 2013: Site User

3. Open a previous version and compare it to the current version.
   a) For the version **1.0** of the document, select the date.
   b) The document opens in Microsoft Word. Observe the warning that appears at the top of the document informing you that the document is a previous version.
   c) In the **Previous Version** warning bar, select **Compare**.

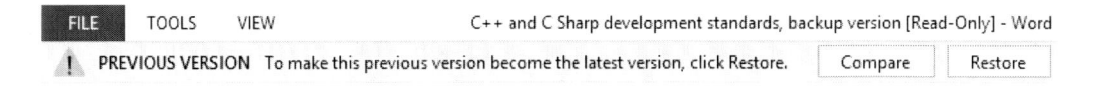

FILE TOOLS VIEW	C++ and C Sharp development standards, backup version [Read-Only] - Word
⚠ PREVIOUS VERSION To make this previous version become the latest version, click Restore.	Compare Restore

   d) The **Compare Result** opens in Microsoft Word.
   e) Close both versions of the **C++ and C Sharp development standards** document and any other open Microsoft Word documents. When you are prompted to save, select **Don't Save**.
   f) Close the **Version History** window and the document preview window.

4. Delete a document.
   a) In the **Team Documents** library, next to **<Your User Name> Resume** select the **Open Menu** button.
   b) In the document preview window, select the **Open Menu** button, and then select **Delete**.
   c) Select **OK** to confirm the deletion.

   > **Note:** Wait for instructor before proceeding beyond this step.

5. Instructor restores deleted documents from Recycle Bin (Instructor Instructions).
   a) Log on as **Develetech\Administrator**.

   > **Note:** Only the instructor performs the following steps.

   b) Open your web browser and browse to **http://sharepoint**.
   c) In **Quick Launch** area, select **Team Documents**.
   d) In the header, select **Settings**, and then select **Site settings**.

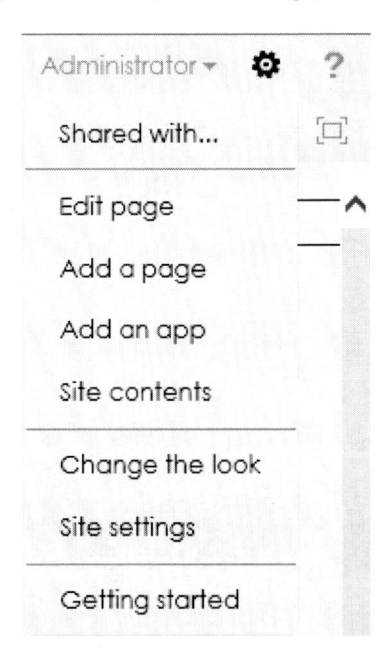

   Administrator ▼ ⚙ ?
   Shared with...
   Edit page
   Add a page
   Add an app
   Site contents
   Change the look
   Site settings
   Getting started

   e) On the **Site settings** page, under **Site Collection Administration**, select **Recycle Bin**.
   f) On the **Recycle Bin** page, allow the class to observe the contents of the Recycle Bin.
   g) Check the check boxes next to the documents you wish to restore, and select **Restore Selection**.

Lesson 5: Integrating with Microsoft Office | Topic B

h) When prompted, select **OK**.

6. Verify the file was restored (Learner Instructions).
   a) In SharePoint, in **Team Documents,** refresh the web page and observe the restored file.

7. Check out documents.
   a) In the **Quick Launch** area, under **Subsites,** select **Project Orange.**
   b) Select **Orange Documents.**
   c) On the **Orange Documents** page, next to **<Your User Name> test cases,** select the **Open Menu** button, and then select **EDIT.**
   d) The document opens in Microsoft Word. Observe the warning at the top of the document that check out is required to modify the document.
   e) Select **Check Out.**

FILE	TOOLS	VIEW	Student2 test cases - Word
CHECK OUT REQUIRED	To modify this server document, you must check it out.		Check Out

   f) Switch to your browser, close the preview window, and refresh the **Orange Documents** page.
   g) Observe the icon next to the document you checked out.

   Student2 test cases   ...   Tuesday at 1:38 PM   student2

   h) Ask another learner to attempt to edit the document you have checked out.

8. Attempt to open a checked out document.
   a) To attempt to open a document that another learner has checked out, in the **Orange Documents** page, next to **<Partner User Name> Test Cases,** select the **Open Menu** button.

   > **Note:** Observe that there is no edit option available on the primary menu of the preview window.

   b) In the preview window, select the **Open Menu** button to open the full document menu. Observe the options on the menu.
   c) Close the preview window.

9. Check your document back in.
   a) Switch to Microsoft Word.
   b) In the document you checked out, select **FILE,** and then select **Info.**

   > **Note:** Observe the actions that you can take on the checked out document. You can check it in, or discard the check out and abandon your changes.

c) Select **Check In.**

Student2 test cases

http://sharepoint » green » Shared Documents

Checked Out Document

No one else can edit this document or view your changes until it is checked in.

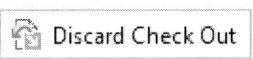

Check In

Discard Check Out

d) In the **Check In** dialog box, under **Version Type**, select **2.0 Major Version (publish)**.
e) Select **OK**.
f) Switch to your browser, refresh the **Orange Documents** page, and observe the change in the document icon.

Student2 test cases ••• About a minute ago student2

Note: Wait for the check in to complete before moving on.

g) Close any open Microsoft Word documents.
h) In the top menu, select **Developer Team Site.**

TOPIC C

Access SharePoint Data from Outlook 2013

Many people use Microsoft Outlook as their primary productivity tool. In effect, Microsoft Outlook becomes the hub they use to access the information they work with the most. In this topic, you will learn how to synchronize information from SharePoint to Microsoft Outlook.

Content That Can Synchronize from SharePoint to Outlook

If you have Microsoft Outlook installed on your local computer, you can synchronize document libraries, calendars, contact lists, and other types of lists from SharePoint to Outlook. This brings the content into Outlook, allowing you to select the library, calendar, or list, and work with the documents or items it contains from Outlook. If Outlook is available offline, you can work on information synchronized from SharePoint while offline, and the information will be updated when you are back online.

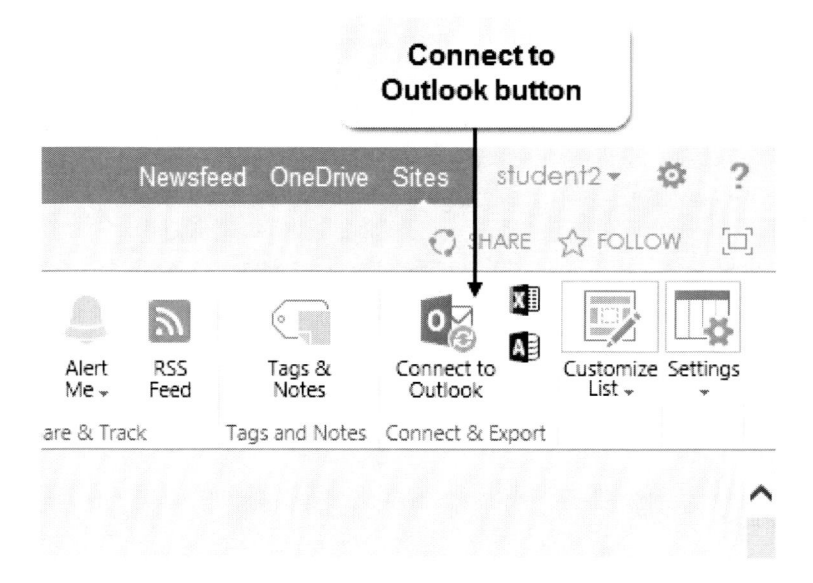

Figure 5-3: The Connect to Outlook button.

Location of Synchronized SharePoint Information in Outlook.

Synchronized calendars, lists, and libraries will appear in the **Outlook Folder** pane. For example, a synchronized calendar would appear under **Other Calendars.** Items from the calendar, list, or library will appear in the **Content** pane. For example, if you synchronized a document library, the documents stored in that library would appear in the **Content** pane. You could then select a document and see a preview of it in the **Reading** pane in Outlook.

> Access the Checklist tile on your CHOICE Course screen for reference information and job aids on How to Synchronize Calendars, Document Libraries and Lists from SharePoint to Outlook.

ACTIVITY 5-3
Synchronizing Calendars, Document Libraries and Lists from SharePoint to Outlook

Before You Begin
You should be logged onto the classroom SharePoint site, and your browser should have the SharePoint Developer Team site home page open.

Scenario
Now that you have access to the content you need in SharePoint, you want to synchronize it with Microsoft Outlook so that you can access the most important and frequently used information directly from Outlook. In this activity, you will synchronize lists and libraries with Outlook and view and access SharePoint items from within Microsoft Outlook.

1. Synchronize a document library with Outlook.
   a) In your web browser, in the **Quick Launch** area, select **Team Documents**.
   b) Select the **C++ and C Sharp developer standard** document.
   c) In the Microsoft Word Web App, select the **EDIT DOCUMENT** tab, and select **Edit in Word**.
   d) The document is opened in Microsoft Word in read-only mode. Minimize Microsoft Word.
   e) In your web browser, a window is open explaining that your document is being opened in Microsoft Word. Select **My document opened successfully, close Word Web App**.

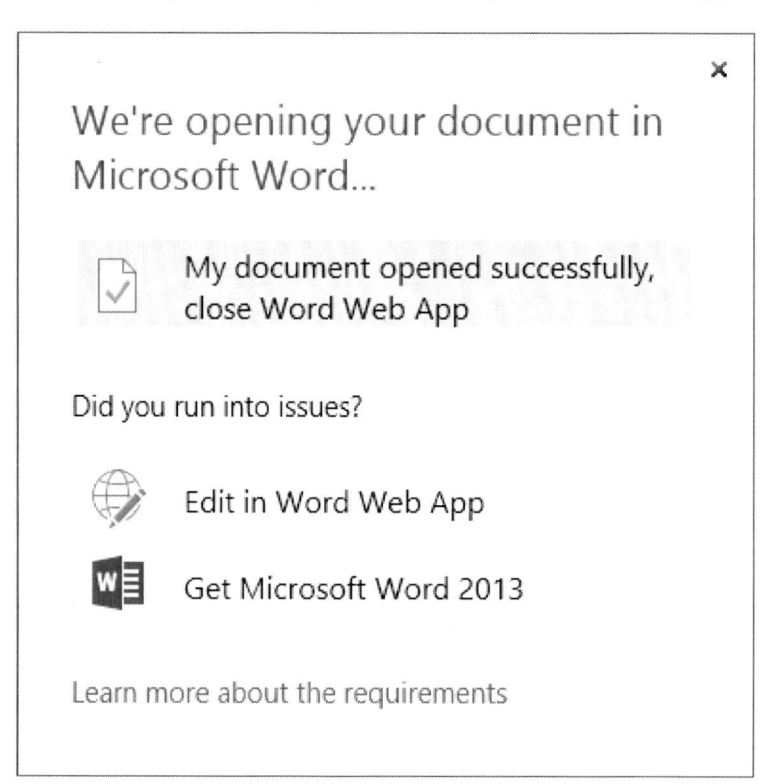

   f) On the **Team Documents** page, in the ribbon, select the **LIBRARY** tab, and then in the **Connect and Export** group, select **Connect to Outlook**.

g) A dialog box appears asking if you wish to allow the website to open Outlook; select **Allow**.
h) If you receive a certificate error, select **Yes**.
i) Microsoft Outlook opens, and a dialog box appears asking if you want to connect the SharePoint document library to Outlook. Select **Yes**.

> **Note:** Outlook might take a few seconds to open. Optionally, you can select Outlook on your taskbar.

2. View the document library in Outlook.
    a) In Microsoft Outlook, in the **Folder** pane, expand **SharePoint Lists,** and select **Developer Team Site - Team Documents.**

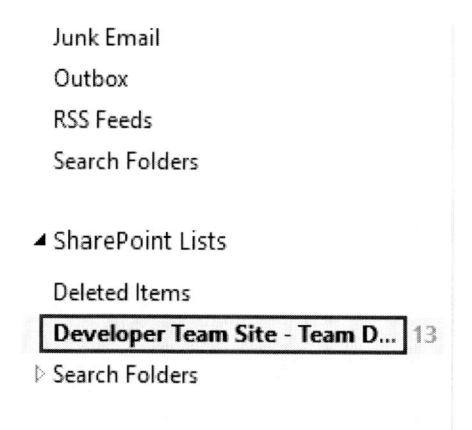

    Junk Email
    Outbox
    RSS Feeds
    Search Folders

    ▲ SharePoint Lists
    Deleted Items
    Developer Team Site - Team D... 13
    ▷ Search Folders

    b) In the **Content** pane, observe that each document from the **Team Documents** library is listed and available.

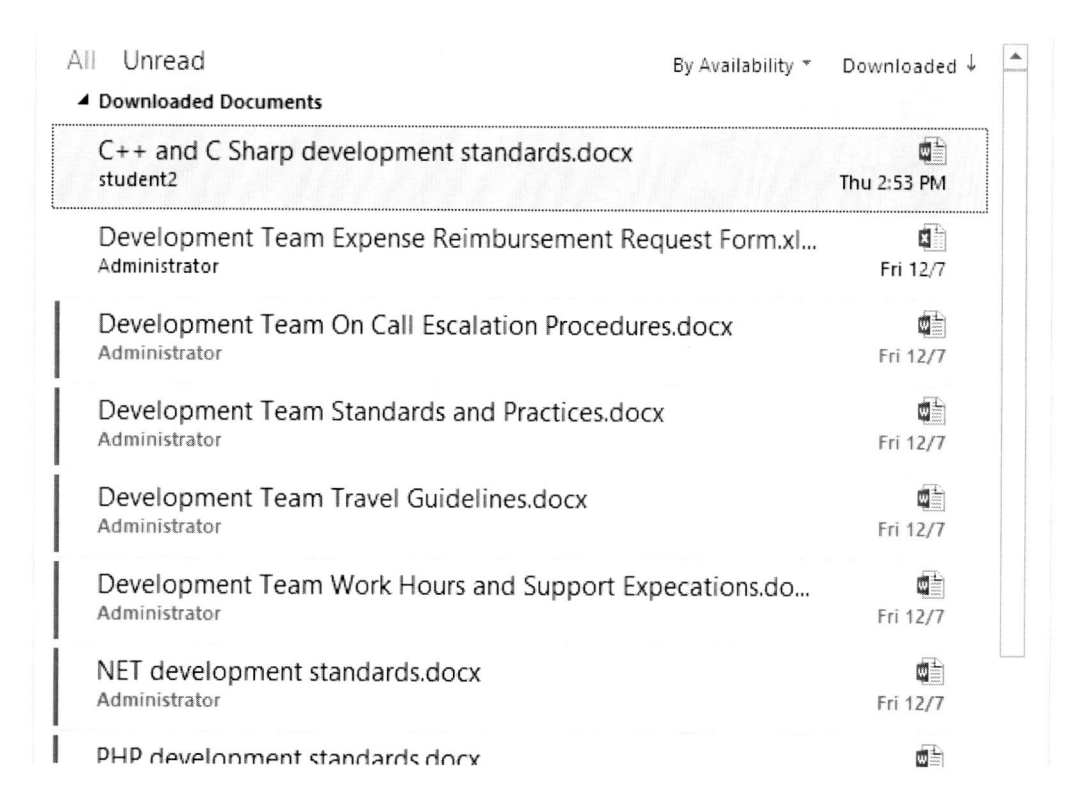

    All Unread   By Availability ▼   Downloaded ↓
    ▲ Downloaded Documents

    C++ and C Sharp development standards.docx
    student2   Thu 2:53 PM

    Development Team Expense Reimbursement Request Form.xl...
    Administrator   Fri 12/7

    Development Team On Call Escalation Procedures.docx
    Administrator   Fri 12/7

    Development Team Standards and Practices.docx
    Administrator   Fri 12/7

    Development Team Travel Guidelines.docx
    Administrator   Fri 12/7

    Development Team Work Hours and Support Expecations.do...
    Administrator   Fri 12/7

    NET development standards.docx
    Administrator   Fri 12/7

    PHP development standards.docx

c) Select the **Development Team Expense Reimbursement Request Form** spreadsheet, and observe the **Reading** pane.

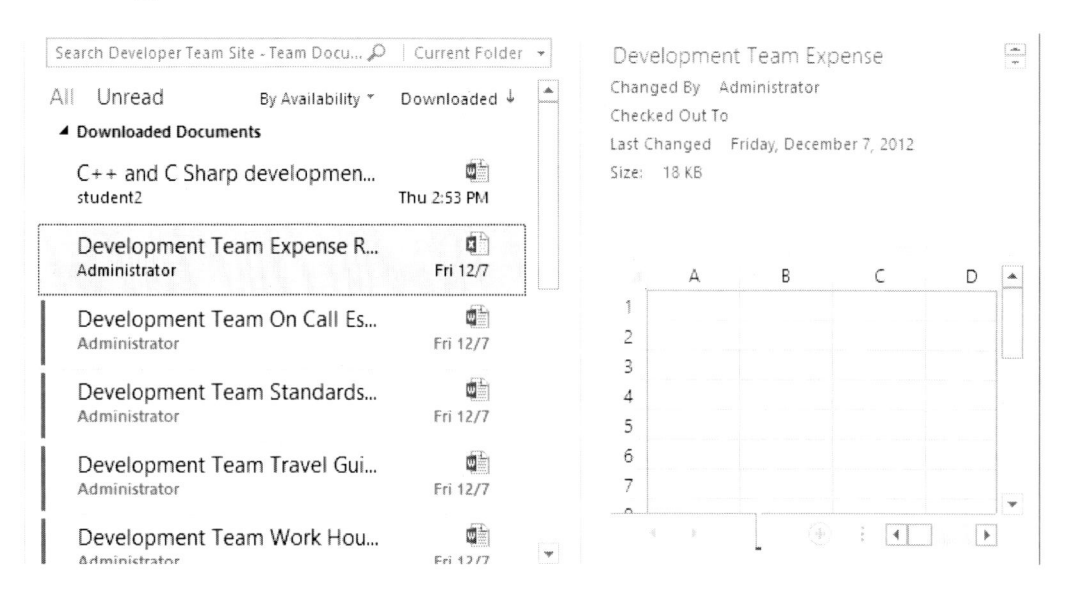

d) Select the **<Your User Name> Resume** document, and observe the **Reading** pane.

3. Edit a document while offline in Outlook.

   a) In the **Content** pane, double-click **<Your User Name> Resume updated** to open this file in Microsoft Word.

   > **Note:** You must open the document to see the **Edit Offline** option.

   b) The document is displayed in Microsoft Word.

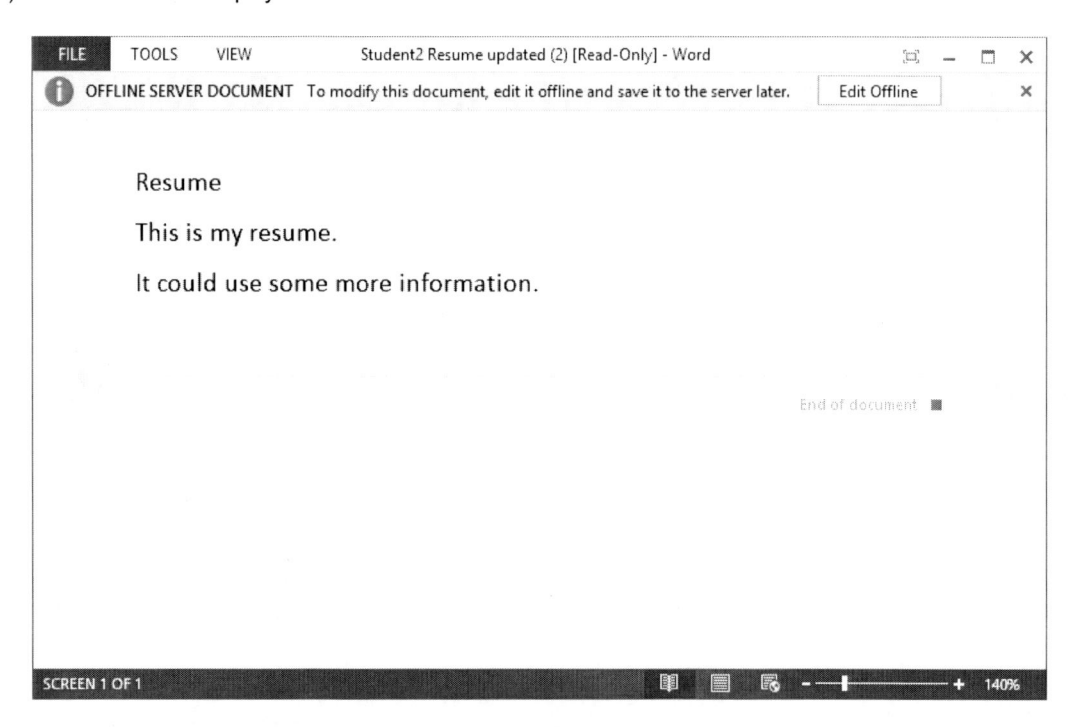

   c) Observe the notification at the top of Microsoft Word. Select **Edit Offline**.
   d) In the **Edit Offline** dialog box, read the message and select **OK**.
   e) In the body of the document, type *Offline Update*

f) Save the document and close Microsoft Word.
g) A prompt appears asking if you would like to update the server, select **Update**.

4. Review the updated document.
    a) In **Microsoft Outlook**, in the **Folder** pane, under your email address, select **Inbox** to return to the Inbox view in Outlook.
    b) Switch to **SharePoint**.
    c) In the **Team Documents** page, select **<Your User Name> Resume updated**.
    d) The document opens in Microsoft Word Web App. Observe that the document is updated with the changes made from Outlook.
    e) Close Microsoft Word Web App.

5. Synchronize a SharePoint calendar in Outlook.
    a) In the **Quick Launch** area, select **Team Calendar**.
    b) On the **Team Calendar** page, on the ribbon, select the **CALENDAR** tab, and in the **Connect & Export** group, select **Connect to Outlook**.
    c) A dialog box appears asking if you wish to allow the website to open Outlook, select **Allow**.
    d) If you receive a certificate error, select **Yes**.
    e) Microsoft Outlook opens, and a dialog box appears asking if you want to connect the SharePoint Calendar to Outlook. Select **Advanced**. If you receive another certificate error message, select **Yes**.

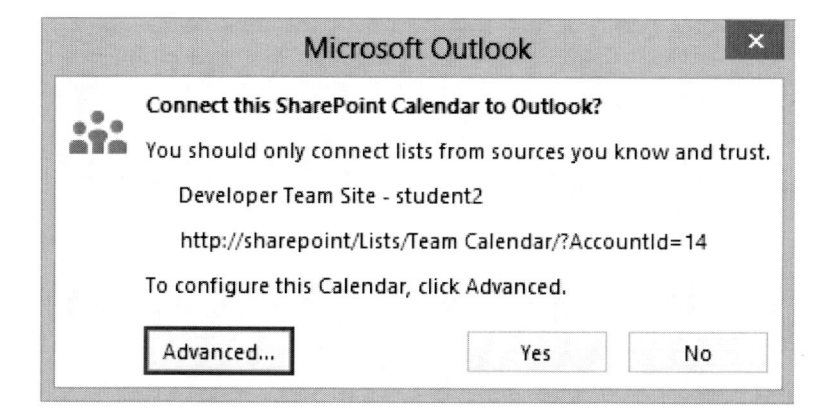

    f) In the **SharePoint List Options** dialog box, observe the SharePoint list options.
    g) Select **OK**.
    h) In the Microsoft Outlook dialog box, select **Yes**.

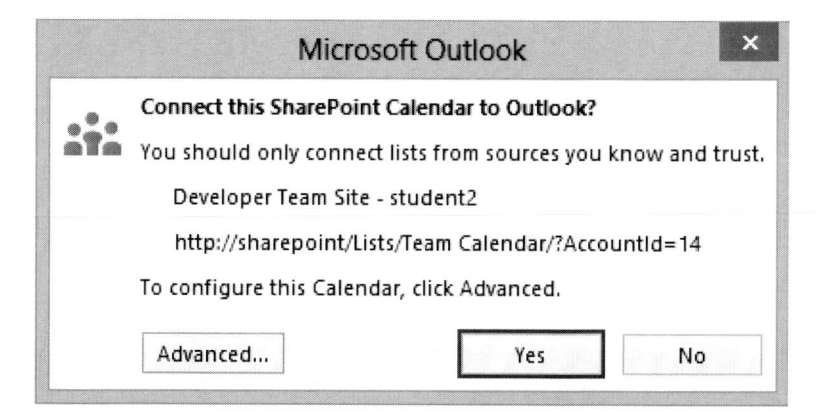

6. View the SharePoint calendar in Outlook.
    a) Observe the Microsoft Outlook calendar interface.

b) In the bottom of the **Folder** pane, see the list of calendars (you might need to scroll down to see them).

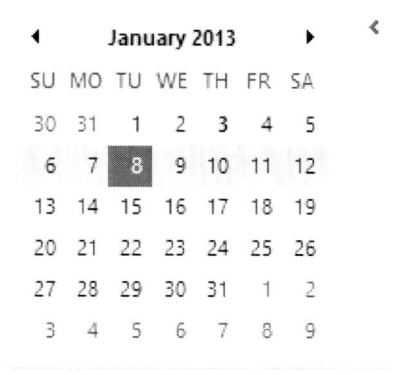

◀   January 2013   ▶

SU	MO	TU	WE	TH	FR	SA
30	31	1	2	3	4	5
6	7	8	9	10	11	12
13	14	15	16	17	18	19
20	21	22	23	24	25	26
27	28	29	30	31	1	2
3	4	5	6	7	8	9

▲ ☑ My Calendars

    ☑ **Calendar**

▷ ☐ Team: ShellyS

▲ ☑ Other Calendars

    ☑ **Developer Team Site - stud...**

> **Note:** If the **Folder** pane is not visible click the **Expand the Folder Pane** button.

c) Under **Other Calendars,** uncheck **Developer Team Site.**
d) Observe how the Calendar view changes.
e) Under **Other Calendars,** check **Developer Team Site.**

f) In the **Folder** pane, in the navigation bar, select **Mail** button to return to the Inbox.

Summary

In this lesson, you learned about the ways in which Microsoft Office integrates with SharePoint. You accessed and saved documents directly in SharePoint from Microsoft Office applications, you used SharePoint version control such as version history and managed previous versions through Microsoft Word, and checked documents out and into SharePoint. You synchronized SharePoint content to Microsoft Outlook and accessed that content inside of Outlook.

What integration points do you feel your organization will use and why?

Are there opportunities to use versioning or document check out/check in within your organization?

> **Note:** Check your LogicalCHOICE Course screen for opportunities to interact with your classmates, peers, and the larger LogicalCHOICE online community about the topics covered in this course or other topics you are interested in. From the Course screen you can also access available resources for a more continuous learning experience.

6 | Working Offline and Remotely with SharePoint

Lesson Time: 40 minutes

Lesson Objectives

In this lesson, you will:

- Synchronize SharePoint libraries and sites, and work with data offline and synchronize it back to SharePoint.

- Access SharePoint from a mobile device.

Lesson Introduction

One of the reasons Microsoft® SharePoint® is a great collaboration tool is because it provides a central place where you can store documents and share information. In order to be effective in today's work environment, however, users need to be able to access files and other information from anywhere, and from their mobile devices, including tablets and smartphones. In addition, users need to be able to work on documents and files even when they cannot access their SharePoint server, and changes made offline need to be synchronized with the server. In this lesson, you will learn how to synchronize SharePoint content for offline use and access SharePoint from a mobile device.

TOPIC A

Synchronize Libraries, Sites, and MySite and Working Offline

The first step in preparing to work offline with SharePoint content is to identify those sites and libraries which have information you will need while you are working offline. In this topic you will learn how to synchronize SharePoint libraries and sites, and how to work with data when you're offline and synchronize it back to SharePoint.

SharePoint 2013 Offline Synchronization Features

SharePoint 2013 allows you to synchronize sites and document libraries for use offline as long as Microsoft® Office is installed on the local system. From any site or document library that you wish to synchronize, you can simply select the **SYNC** button from the ribbon to synchronize the folder. The site or library is synchronized to OneDrive® Pro, and is made available under favorites on your local system. You can work offline with sites and documents that you have synchronized and changes will be synchronized back to SharePoint when you come back online.

Figure 6-1: The SharePoint SYNC button.

Managing Offline Synchronization from the Client

After you have synchronized libraries and sites, an icon appears in the system tray. You can right-click the icon to open a SharePoint folder, sync a new library, stop syncing a folder, and to initiate or pause syncing.

> Access the Checklist tile on your CHOICE Course screen for reference information and job aids on How to Synchronize Libraries, Sites, Your MySite and Work Offline with Content.

ACTIVITY 6-1
Synchronizing Libraries, Sites, and Your MySite and Working Offline with Content

Before You Begin
You should be logged onto the classroom SharePoint site, and your browser should have the Team Documents library page open.

Scenario
You've had a good first day at Develetech, but you want access to the documents that you're most interested in on your laptop computer so that you can work from the home, or while travelling. To do that, you will use the synchronization feature in SharePoint 2013 to synchronize selected libraries, sites, and your MySite for offline use. You will then test working with the documents offline, and synchronizing the changes back up to SharePoint.

1. Synchronize the Team Documents library.
    a) In the **Team Documents** library, in the ribbon, select **SYNC**.

    b) The **Microsoft OneDrive Pro** dialog box displays asking if you wish to sync the **Team Documents** library. Observe the location where you can find the documents.

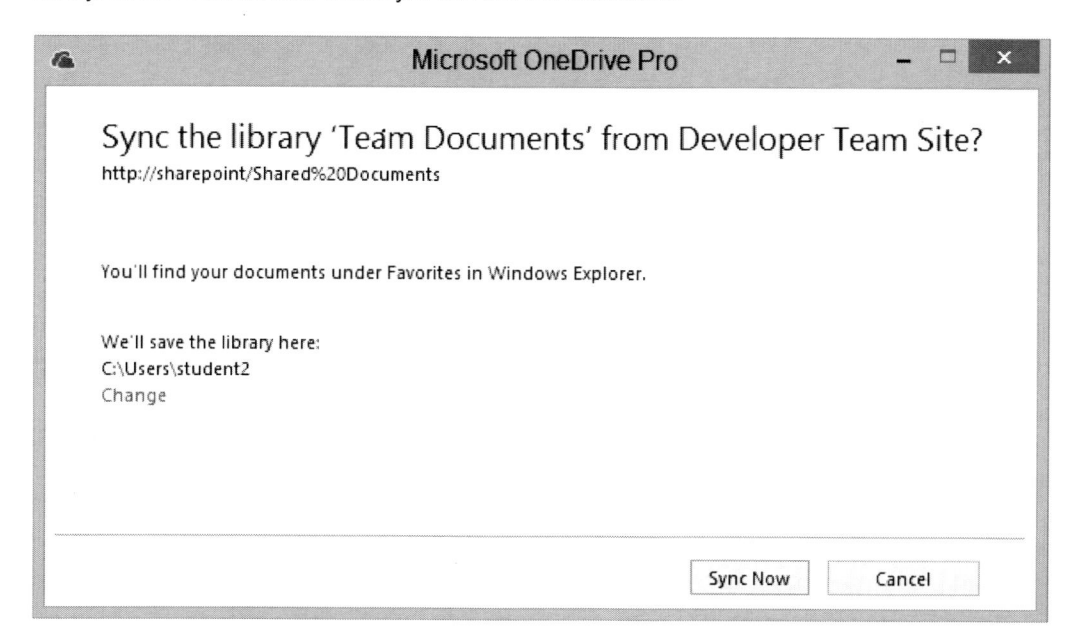

    c) Select **Sync Now**. The files will sync to your local system.
    d) When synchronization is complete, observe the location of the files on your local system. Select **Show my files**.

e) A Windows Explorer window opens, showing the synchronized files.

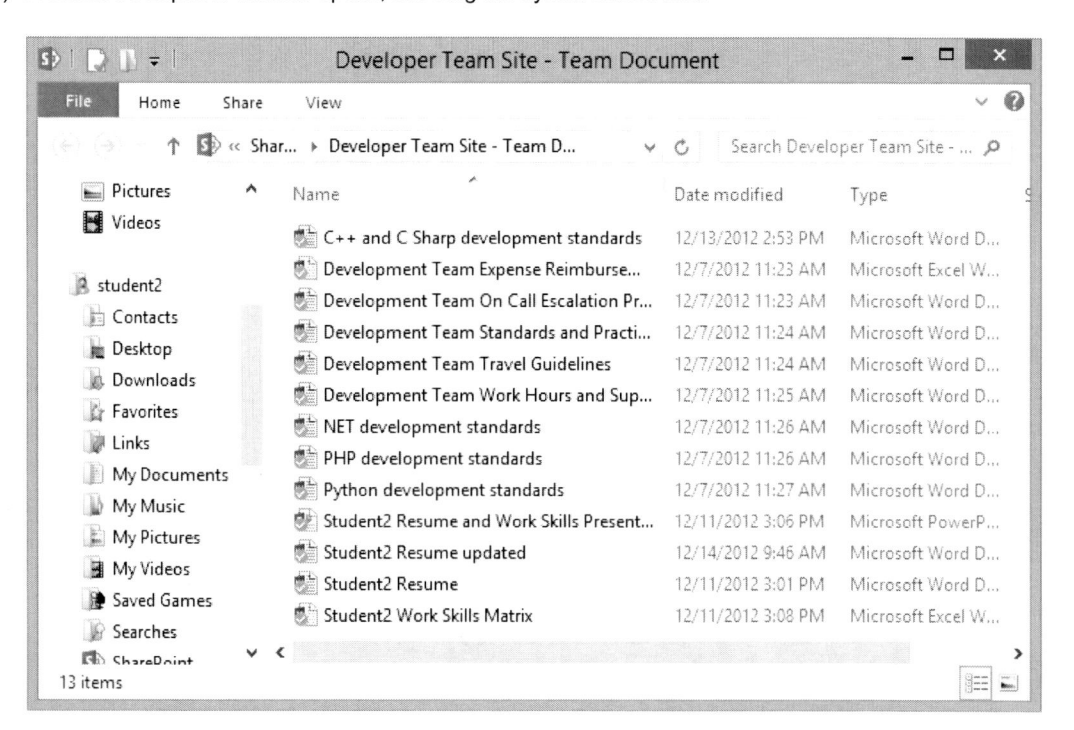

> **Note:** Leave Windows Explorer open because you will come back to it later.

2. Synchronize the Project Orange Site.
   a) Switch to SharePoint, in the **Quick Launch** area, select **Project Orange**.
   b) On the **Project Orange** page, in the ribbon select **SYNC**.
   c) The **Microsoft OneDrive Pro** dialog box displays.
   d) Select **Sync Now**. When the synchronization completes, close the **Microsoft OneDrive Pro** dialog box.

3. Synchronize your MySite.
   a) In the header bar, select **OneDrive**.
   b) On the **OneDrive Pro Documents** page, in the ribbon, select **SYNC**.
   c) In the **Microsoft OneDrive Pro** dialog box, select **Sync Now**. When synchronization completes, close the **Microsoft OneDrive Pro** dialog box.
   d) In the browser window, select the **back** button.

4. Disable your network interface.
   a) Minimize all open windows.

   > **Note:** You will disable your network interface to simulate being offline.

b) On the Windows 8 status bar, right-click the network icon, and select **Open Network and Sharing Center**.

> **Note:** If your computer is using a wireless network adapter, right-click the signal status bars and select **Open Network and Sharing Center**.

c) In the **Network and Sharing Center** window, select **Change adapter settings**.

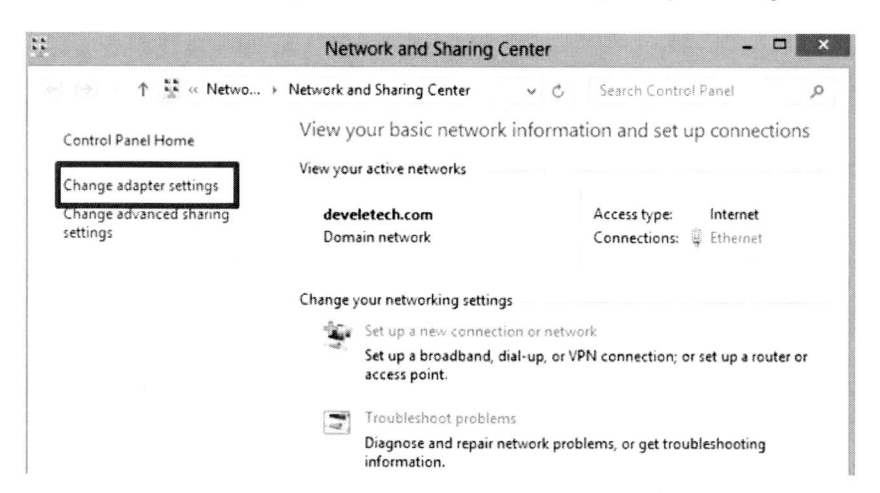

d) In the **Network Connections** window, right-click the network adaptor icon and select **Disable**.

e) A **User Account Control** dialog box will display asking for administrator credentials. In the **User Name** box type *administrator* and in the **Password** box, type *P@ssw0rd12*, and select **Yes**.

> **Note:** The instructor will provide you with the administrator ID's password for this step.

f) The network adapter will change color and show as disabled.

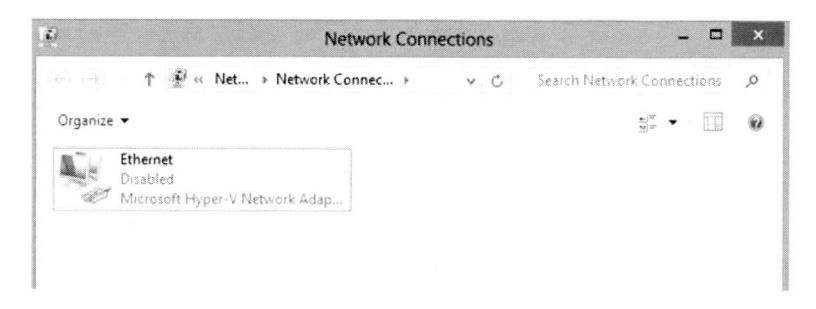

g) Minimize the **Network Connections** window.

> **Note:** You will need to keep the **Network Connections** window open to enable the network adapter later.

h) Close the **Network and Sharing Center** window.

5. Observe offline documents and files.
   a) Switch to Windows Explorer.

b) In the **Tree** pane, under **Favorites** select **SharePoint**. In the **Details** pane, observe the folders.

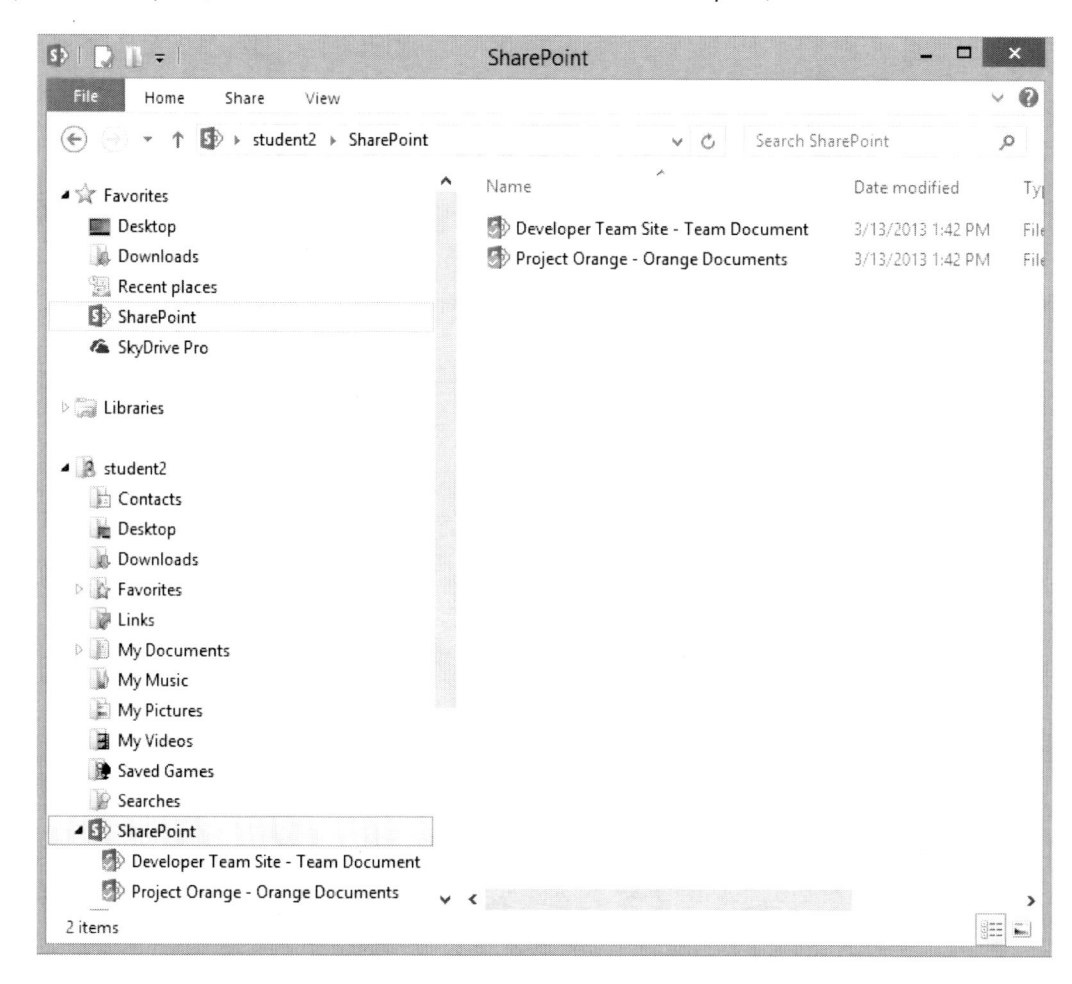

c) In the **Tree** pane, under **SharePoint**, select **Developer Team Site - Team Document**.

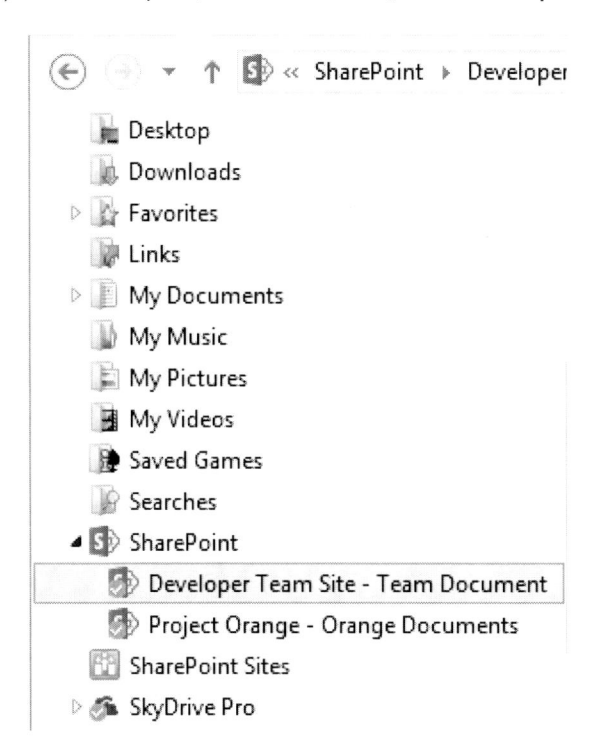

d) In the **Details** pane, observe the files and note the green check on the file icons, which indicates that the files are synchronized with SharePoint.

6. Edit files while offline.
   a) Open the **<Your User Name> Resume updated** document.
   b) The document opens in Microsoft Word. Note the message that informs you that the document is offline.

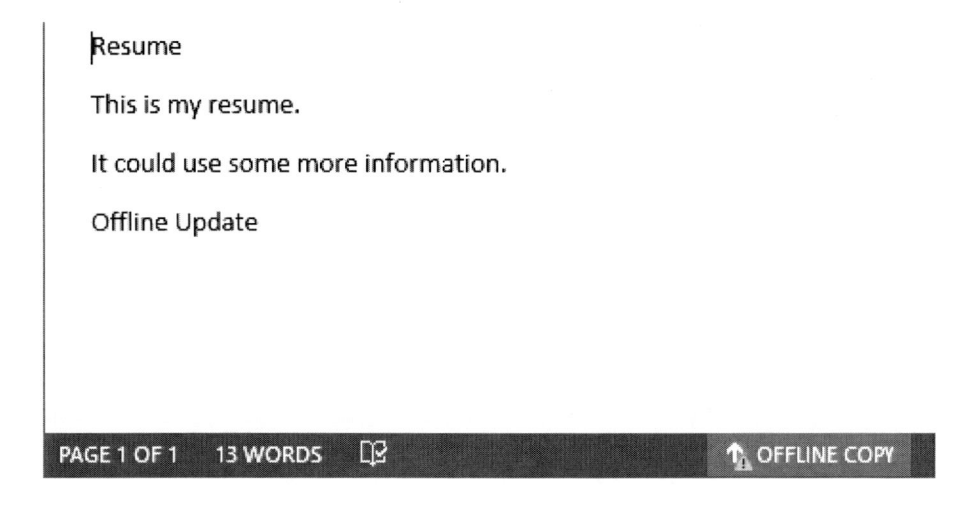

   Resume

   This is my resume.

   It could use some more information.

   Offline Update

   c) In the body of the document, under **Offline Update,** type *Offline Update 2*
   d) Save the document and close Microsoft Word.
   e) If an **Uploading to SharePoint** dialog box displays as Microsoft Word attempts to contact the SharePoint server, wait for the dialog box to close.

f) In Windows Explorer, observe the **<Your User Name> Resume updated** file. Observe how the green check has been replaced by a blue synchronization symbol.

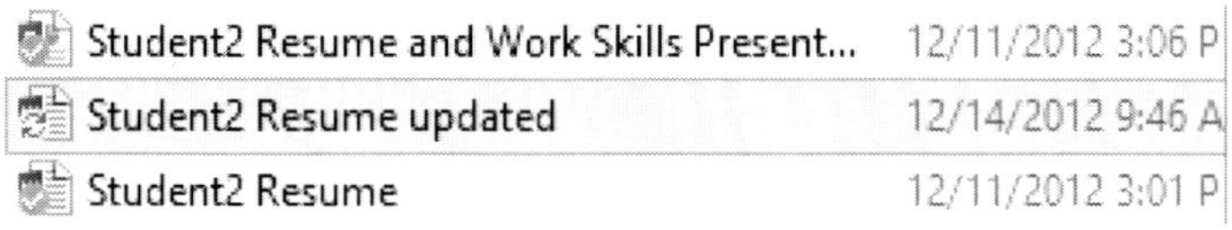

7. Enable your network adapter to come back online.
   a) Switch to the **Network Connections** window.

   > **Note:** You will enable your network interface to come back online.

   b) In the **Network Connections** window, right-click the network adapter icon and select **Enable**.
   c) A **User Account Control** dialog box will display asking for administrator credentials, in the **User Name** box, type *administrator* and in the **Password** box, type *P@ssw0rd12*, and select **Yes**.

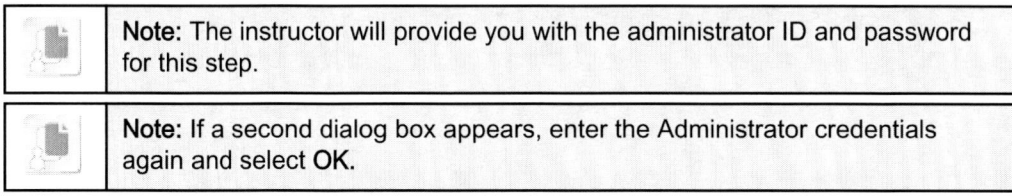

   > **Note:** The instructor will provide you with the administrator ID and password for this step.

   > **Note:** If a second dialog box appears, enter the Administrator credentials again and select **OK**.

   d) The network adapter will change color and show as enabled.

   e) Close the **Network Connections** window.

8. Review offline file synchronization status after coming online.
   a) In Windows Explorer, observe the **<Your User Name> Resume updated** file. The file should synchronize with the SharePoint server shortly after your system comes back online.

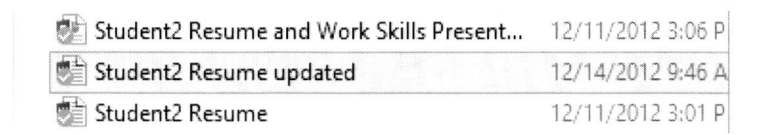

   b) When the **<Your User Name> Resume updated** is showing as synchronized, close Windows Explorer.
   c) In SharePoint, on the Top menu bar, select **Developer Team Site**.
   d) On the **Developer Team Site**, in the **Quick Launch** area, select **Team Documents**.
   e) on the **Team Documents** page, select **<Your User Name> Resume updated**.
   f) The document opens in Microsoft Word Web App. Verify your changes have been saved to SharePoint.
   g) Close Microsoft Word Web App.

TOPIC B

Work from a Mobile Device

When you are away from your PC and need access to SharePoint, you can use a mobile device, such as a tablet or smartphone, to view and update documents. In this topic, you will learn how to access SharePoint from a mobile device.

SharePoint 2013 Mobile Device Access Features

SharePoint provides a mobile formatted version of your SharePoint site to allow you to more easily access the site from a mobile device. The mobile version of the site can be accessed by typing a **/m** after the URL of the SharePoint site. For example, to access the mobile formatted version of the classroom SharePoint site you would type ***http://sharepoint/m***. In fact, when you create a new list view, you can choose if the view will be available in mobile mode from the **Create or Edit List View** page. Microsoft is also releasing SharePoint apps for iOS®, Android™, and Windows® Phone devices to allow for a more robust and consistent user experience across major mobile platforms.

> **Access the Checklist tile on your CHOICE Course screen for reference information and job aids on How to Access SharePoint Sites and Content from a Mobile Device.**

ACTIVITY 6-2
Accessing SharePoint Sites and Content from a Mobile Device

Before You Begin
You should be logged onto the classroom SharePoint site, and your browser should have the Team Documents library page open.

Scenario
You're travelling today, and just got a call from your supervisor. She's asked you to review the **C++ and C Sharp development standards** document as soon as possible, so you're going to try to use your mobile device while at the airport.

1. Browse to the SharePoint site from the mobile device.

    > **Note:** This activity requires a Wi-Fi connected smartphone or tablet that can access the classroom SharePoint server. Optionally, you can observe the SharePoint mobile interface by browsing to http://<*IP address of the SharePoint server*>/m.

    a) Verify that you are connected to a network that can communicate with the SharePoint server.
    b) Obtain the IP address of the SharePoint server from your instructor.
    c) Open the browser on the mobile device.

    > **Note:** If you are not using a mobile device, open your web browser.

    d) In the address bar of the browser type, *http://<IP Address of the SharePoint Server>* and attempt to open the SharePoint site.

    > **Note:** If you are not using a mobile device, browse to **http://sharepoint/m**.

    e) When prompted to log on, provide your user name and password.
    f) Observe the SharePoint device display.

2. Navigation to Team documents.
    a) Select the **Site** icon on the upper-right portion of the page display.
    b) From the menu, select **Site Contents**.
    c) One the **Site Contents** page, select **Team Documents** to open the library.
    d) Observe the documents available on the **Team Documents** page.

3. Open the **C++ and C Sharp developer standards** document.
    a) On the **Team Documents** page, select the **C++ and C Sharp developer standards** document.
    b) Observe the document on your mobile device.

    > **Note:** If you are not using a mobile device, observe the document on your client PC.

Summary

In this lesson, you synchronized sites and document libraries and worked with files while offline. You saw interface icons that showed when files were in sync and out of sync, and you accessed the mobile version of your SharePoint site.

In what cases would you work offline with SharePoint?

What are some potential issues and problems with working offline?

> **Note:** Check your LogicalCHOICE Course screen for opportunities to interact with your classmates, peers, and the larger LogicalCHOICE online community about the topics covered in this course or other topics you are interested in. From the Course screen you can also access available resources for a more continuous learning experience.

Course Follow-Up

Congratulations! You have completed the *Microsoft® SharePoint® 2013: Site User* course. You have successfully accessed, edited, and saved documents and data in a collaboration space and accessed the information of your learning partners.

The ability to collaborate effectively and efficiently is important to success in the workplace and on teams and will continue to be a critical skill in an increasingly connected world. The knowledge of and ability to use SharePoint's collaboration, communication, and social network features will allow you to be more productive on a day-to-day basis, and allow you to work more effectively with team members in your organization.

What's Next?

Microsoft® SharePoint® 2013: Site Owner is the next course in this series. In that course, you will create, and customize a SharePoint site. You will add libraries and lists, configure them, and assign permissions to them. You will configure site layout, site search, and site settings. You will enable advanced library and list features, such as content approval, and configure content roll-up applications.

You are encouraged to explore SharePoint further by actively participating in any of the social media forums set up by your instructor or training administrator through the **Social Media** tile on the LogicalCHOICE Course screen.

A | Microsoft Office SharePoint 2013 Exam 77-419

Selected Logical Operations courseware addresses Microsoft Office Specialist (MOS) certification skills for Microsoft Office 2013. The following table indicates where SharePoint 2013 skills that are tested on Exam 77-419 are covered in the Logical Operations Microsoft Office SharePoint 2013 series of courses.

Objective Domain	Covered In
1. Create and Format Content	
1.1. Navigate SharePoint Hierarchy	
1.1.1. Using Quick Launch	Part 1, Topic 1-B
1.1.2. Using All Site Content	Part 2
1.1.3. Using breadcrumb trails	Part 3
1.1.4. Adding content to Quick Launch	Part 2
1.1.5. Using Content and Structure for Navigation	Part 1, Topic 1-B
1.2. Manage Lists and Libraries	
1.2.1. Creating Lists	Part 2
1.2.2. Creating Libraries	Part 2
1.2.3. Editing properties for new items	Part 1, Topic 2-B
1.2.4. Enabling email notifications on lists or libraries	Part 3
1.2.5. Providing shortcuts to a mobile site URL	Part 2
1.2.6. Managing document templates	Part 2
1.2.7. Managing list views	Part 1, Topic 3-A
1.2.8. Creating alerts on lists or libraries	Part 1, Topic 2-B
1.2.9. Using ratings	Part 2
1.2.10. Adding columns	Part 3
1.2.11. Adding content validation	Part 2
1.2.12. Managing column properties	Part 2
1.3. Manage List Items	

Objective Domain	Covered In
1.3.1. Creating new list items	Part 1, Topic 1-A
1.3.2. Editing content	Part 1, Topic 3-A
1.3.3. Deleting list items or documents	Part 1, Topic 3-A
1.3.4. Versioning list items	Part 1, Topic 5-B
1.3.5. Publishing Assets	Part 2
1.3.6. Managing existing workflows	Part 3
1.3.7. Uploading documents	Part 1, Topic 2-A
1.3.8. Creating and managing announcements	Part 1, Topic 3-A
1.3.9. Collaborating with Microsoft Office assets (calendars, spreadsheets, web apps)	Part 1, Topics 2-A, 5-A, 5-C
1.4. Manage Document Sets	
1.4.1. Adding documents to document sets	Part 3
1.4.2. Creating document sets	Part 3
1.4.3. Activating and deactivating documents sets	Part 3
2. Manage SharePoint Sites	
2.1. Manage Pages	
2.1.1. Creating new site pages	Part 2
2.2.1. Using templates	Part 2
2.1.2. Editing and deleting existing site pages	Part 2
2.2. Perform Administrative Tasks on Sites and Workspaces	
2.2.1. Creating new sites or workspaces using templates	Part 2
2.2.2. Configuring site or workspace structures	Part 2
2.2.3. Configuring the content organizer	Part 3
2.2.4. Displaying a list of all user alerts	Part 3
2.2.5. Modifying look and feel	Part 2
2.2.6. Recovering assets (lists, libraries, documents and list items)	Part 1, Topic 5-B
2.2.7. Using document and meeting workspaces	Featured not present in SharePoint 2013 - see similar functionality in Part 2
2.2.8. Viewing site web analytics	Part 2
2.2.9. Viewing detailed reports	Part 2
2.3. Manage Web Parts on a Page	
2.3.1. Adding Web Parts	Part 2
2.3.2. Configuring Web Parts	Part 2
2.3.3. Hiding or removing Web Parts	Part 2
2.3.4. Exporting or importing Web Parts	Part 3

Objective Domain	Covered In
2.4. Manage Content Types	
2.4.1. Associating content types to lists	Part 3
2.4.2. Extending the columns of content types	Part 3
2.4.3. Creating custom content types	Part 3
2.5 Manage Users and Groups	
2.5.1. Creating groups	Part 2
2.5.2. Managing groups	Part 2
2.5.3. Managing user access	Part 2
2.5.4. Managing group permissions	Part 2
3. Participate in User Communities	
3.1. Configure My Site	
3.1.1. Adding keywords	Part 1, Topic 4-B
3.1.2. Adding colleagues	Featured not present in SharePoint 2013 - see similar functionality in Topic 4-B
3.1.3. Selecting themes	Part 2
3.1.4. Configuring the Colleague Tracker web part	Featured not present in SharePoint 2013 - see similar functionality in Part 2
3.1.5. Configuring RSS feeds	Part 3
3.1.6. Configuring My Profile	Part 1, Topic 4-A
3.2. Collaborate through My Site	
3.2.1. Updating Profile Status	Part 1, Topic 4-A
3.2.2. Sharing Pictures in My Site	Part 1, Topic 4-A
3.2.3. Managing personal documents	Part 1, Topic 4-B
3.2.4. Sharing documents in My Site	Part 1, Topic 4-B
3.2.5. Browsing the organization hierarchy	Part 3
3.2.6. Adding Web Parts to My Site	Part 3
3.3. Add Tags and Notes to Content	
3.3.1. Adding notes to the note board for lists or libraries	Part 1, Topic 4-B
3.3.2. Adding tags for lists libraries	Part 1, Topic 4-B
3.3.3. Rating items	Part 2
3.3.4. Using tag clouds	Part 3
3.3.5. Reviewing tags on My Site	Part 1, Topic 4-B
4. Configure and Consume Search Results	
4.1. Perform Search Administration at the Site Level	
4.1.1. Configuring searchable columns	Part 3
4.1.2. Configuring list searches	Part 3

Objective Domain	Covered In
4.1.3. Configuring site search visibility	Part 2
4.2. View Search Results	
4.2.1. Using Best Bet results	Part 2
4.2.2. Using the Refinement Panel	Part 2
4.2.3. Using Alerts and RSS feeds with search results	Part 3
4.2.4. Previewing documents	Part 1, Topic 2-A
4.3. Perform Advanced Searches	
4.3.1. Using Boolean operators in searches	Part 3
4.3.2. Using wild cards in searches	Part 2
4.3.3. Using property searches	Part 2
4.3.4. Using Phonetic searches	Part 3
4.3.5. Using People Search	Part 2
4.3.6. Using advanced searches	Part 2

Glossary

collaboration technology
A platform that stores and provides centralized access to information such as documents, lists, media content and other data that a team of workers need. In addition to providing centralized access to this information, it provides document management, integration with software applications and tools used by team members, and other capabilities that make information sharing easier.

Enterprise Keywords
Words or phrases that people use to search for information in a SharePoint site. These are stored in a database called the Managed Team Store. Users can associate them with documents to allow other users to find those documents when the keywords are searched for.

following
Allows you to mark a site, document, person, or other item of interest so that you are notified in your Newsfeed and the other hubs of your personal sites when items you follow are changed or updated.

Gantt Chart
A Gantt Chart is a bar chart that shows graphically how long tasks will take over time. The chart illustrates the start and end dates of tasks so it is easier to visually see how long tasks will take. Gantt Charts are often used to track and visualize tasks as part of projects. The Gantt Chart was developed by Henry Gantt.

hashtags
A form of tag available in SharePoint 2013 written as #tag, and pronounced hashtag. These tags are used the same way tags are used on social networks. You can include a hashtag in a post on your Newsfeed or in a community site to assign keywords that categorize the posts. You can follow hashtags from your Newsfeed to stay current on posts and discussions of interest.

header
A SharePoint navigation component that spans the top of the SharePoint page and contains several navigation elements, including buttons for Newsfeed, OneDrive, Sites, the logged in account, Settings, and Help.

list views
Defines how the items in the list are displayed and may include specific columns, organized in a particular order, filtering or grouping options, and may provide other visualizations such as a calendar for viewing schedules, or Gantt Chart for viewing project tasks. Every list has at least one view. List views may be customized or created to display list data in many different ways.

Newsfeed
One of the hub pages that is part of each user's personal site. It provides a personal status form showing current activities and updates on information, sites and people that are being followed.

Office Web Apps
Online versions of Microsoft Word, Excel, PowerPoint, and OneNote that are designed to allow users to view and edit Office documents from anywhere using a web browser. Office Web Apps integrate with Microsoft SharePoint providing enhanced features for document libraries including the ability to view, share and edit documents from PCs, tablets, and smartphones over the web.

OneDrive Pro
One of the hub pages that is part of each user's personal site. It is a place to create, store, and organize personal documents and files allowing documents to be shared with colleagues, and synchronized so that they are available while offline.

page section
The area of the page in a SharePoint site, to the right of the Quick Launch area, under the ribbon. The page section contains the content for that page in the SharePoint site. It may contain one or more SharePoint lists, libraries, apps, text or media depending on how content is laid out for the site.

permission levels
Rights that are granted to users or groups that provide access to, and allow you to perform actions in a SharePoint site. Administrators can assign default permissions to users and groups, or may choose to customize permissions.

personal sites
Called MySites in previous versions of SharePoint, these are a personal collaboration space, that allows users to quickly access sites, documents and people of interest, and to share documents for collaboration. Personal sites are associated with login accounts and are made up of three hub pages: Newsfeed, OneDrive, and Sites.

Quick Launch
A SharePoint navigation component that resides on the upper-left portion of the page, next to the page section and below the ribbon. It provides several links to libraries, lists, and pages within the site and allows you navigate to those areas quickly.

ribbon
A SharePoint navigation component that resides on the SharePoint page below the header and contains tabs, buttons, and other elements that vary depending on permissions and context. Ribbon elements allow you to perform tasks in SharePoint without the need for extensive navigation.

SharePoint
Microsoft's web-based business collaboration platform. This is a software product that allows people to share and collaborate on documents and other information, as well as communicate with each other. It stores documents, list information, calendar information, and media content in a central web-based location. It also provides access control, content management and organizations, file versioning as well as options for checking content in and out. It provides common social networking features allowing teams to collaborate more effectively in the workplace.

SharePoint columns
Content structures that contain the data stored in SharePoint lists, and are similar to fields in a database.

SharePoint groups
Groups that are associated with user accounts to provide access to SharePoint sites, features and capabilities through permissions levels. There are three groups that are provided by default: Visitors, Members, and Owners. Site administrators can create other groups.

SharePoint libraries
A type of content store in SharePoint that may contain documents, spreadsheets, presentations, pictures, media, or other data files. They are centrally accessible and provide access control and document management capabilities.

SharePoint lists
Content structures that organize, store, and track information about a group of similar items such as contact, calendar, or other information. The information is entered and edited through forms, and is stored in the SharePoint database. SharePoint provides several built-in lists and you can also create custom lists.

SharePoint profile
Stores information about you associated with a user login and allows other users to learn about the user. It contains basic information such as your name, department, title and manager, provides contact information such as email address, phone numbers and address, and allows users to share more about their past projects, skills, schools, interest and other personal data.

SharePoint sites
Websites that run on a SharePoint server, and offer the collaboration features and capabilities provided by SharePoint.

tagging
To associate keywords or phrases with information to allow people to find that information when they search using those familiar terms. In SharePoint you can tag sites, documents, and posts to make it easy for other people to find them, or to make it easier to track content and be notified when it is updated.

Index

A
alerts *38*
apps *15*, *27*

B
blogs *96*

C
collaboration technology *2*
columns *50*

D
document check in and check out *110*
document properties *38*
document versioning *109*

E
Enterprise Keywords *37*, *38*

F
following *84*

H
hashtags *85*
header *11*

I
integration with Office 2013 *28*, *106*
interface elements *10*

L
libraries
    adding folders and documents *26*
    types of *26*
    views *62*
lists
    display styles *64*
    filtering options and operators *71*
    grouping options *72*
    modification options *55*
    types of *50*
list view
    audience *62*
    default views *63*
    settings *63*
    types *62*, *63*

M
Microsoft Office Web Apps
    integration with SharePoint *28*
Microsoft Outlook
    synchronize content to *117*
mobile devices
    access features *133*
    views *62*

N
Newsfeed *86*

O
OneDrive Pro *86*

P

page section *14*
personal sites
    hub pages *84*
profile
    access permissions *81*
    editing *80*

Q

Quick Launch area *13*

R

recovery of deleted items *110*
ribbon *12*

S

search features *37*
SharePoint 2013
    description *2*
    groups *4*
    permission levels *4*
    sites *3*
    versions *3*
site hierarchy *9*
Sites page *87*
synchronization
    offline features *126*

T

tagging *85*
team sites
    purpose of *9*

U

UI *10*
user interface, *See* UI

091107S rev 1.3
ISBN-13 978-1-4246-2124-8
ISBN-10 1-4246-2124-0